Georgiana Hill

A History of English Dress from the Saxon Period to the Present Day

Vol. 2

Georgiana Hill

A History of English Dress from the Saxon Period to the Present Day
Vol. 2

ISBN/EAN: 9783337101589

Printed in Europe, USA, Canada, Australia, Japan

Cover: Foto ©ninafisch / pixelio.de

More available books at **www.hansebooks.com**

A HISTORY

OF

ENGLISH DRESS

*FROM THE SAXON PERIOD TO THE
PRESENT DAY.*

BY

GEORGIANA HILL,

AUTHOR OF "MUNDUS MULIEBRIS."

IN TWO VOLUMES.

VOL. II.

LONDON:
RICHARD BENTLEY AND SON,
Publishers in Ordinary to Her Majesty the Queen.
1893.

(All rights reserved.)

CONTENTS.

THE EIGHTEENTH CENTURY.

CHAPTER I.

Transition from seventeenth to eighteenth century—Servile copying of French fashions—Similarity to the fashions of the sixteenth century ... 3

CHAPTER II.

The reign of the wig—How the wig came in—The wig in France— Powder— Skill of French *perruquiers*— Varieties of wigs worn in England—Lord Bolingbroke and the tie-wig—Cost of wigs—How wigs were stolen —Decline of the wig—Petition of wig-makers—The powder tax—Wigs discarded after French Revolution ... 9

CHAPTER III.

Head-dresses—The "Commode"—Origin of the "Fontange"—Sudden fall of the high head-dress—Its reappearance — Art of preparing "heads"— Dispute between two *friseurs*—Hats—Various styles of coiffure —Caps—Feathers and their inconvenience—Change of style—Hair *à la Grecque* ... 31

CHAPTER IV.

LADIES' DRESS.

The hoop—Its origin—French ladies and their hoops—Inconvenience of hoops in London streets—General fashion of dress—How we procured Parisian fashions—Patching and face-painting—How a lady lost her eyebrows—Narrow "shapes" and tight lacing—The polonaise and sacque—The fan and its uses—The muff—Sudden change of fashion—Clinging gowns—Popularity of muslins—Dress modelled on classic costume—Mixture of styles 63

CHAPTER V.

GENTLEMEN'S DRESS.

Elaboration of a gentleman's toilet—Coats and cravats—The beau—Beau Nash and Beau Brummel—The fashions ridiculed—The macaronies—The muff—Wearing of swords—Seaside fashions—Changes—Introduction of plainer style ... 104

CHAPTER VI.

Court dress—Its formality—No improvements suggested by sovereigns—Costliness and splendour of some Court costumes—"Birthday" dresses—Jewellery—Lace and aprons—Conservative character of Court dress—Fashionable amusements ... 133

CHAPTER VII.

Military dress—Wigs and cocked hats—Lace cravats—Uniforms more settled—Colours and shapes—Cost of military clothing—Unpopularity of the Army—Abuses in Army and Navy 156

CHAPTER VIII.

COSTUMES OF THE COMMONALTY.

London fashions in the country—General dress of the middle classes—Umbrellas: their introduction—Costume of the fashionable world copied by the commonalty—Costume of certain callings ... 164

CHAPTER IX.

Trade and commerce—The silk trade—Lustrings and *à la mode* silks—Smuggling—Prohibition against wearing of Indian calicoes—Lace smuggled in large quantities—The linen trade—Cotton—New machines—The woollen trade—Prosperity of Norwich—The glove trade—The policy of protection 185

THE NINETEENTH CENTURY.

CHAPTER I.

1800–1830.

Rise of the Empire modes—Some eccentricities of costume—Influence of politics on dress—Fanciful costumes—Fashions after the fall of the Empire—Growing plainness in male attire 211

CHAPTER II.

1830–1850.

Big sleeves—Pelerines—Hair-dressing and head-gear—Colours—Out-door costume—Male costume—The chimney-pot hat 238

CHAPTER III.

1850–1870.

Shapeless style of costume—The crinoline—Substitutes for the crinoline—General fashions—Jewellery—Trimmings—Tight lacing—Fall of the crinoline ... 255

CHAPTER IV.

1870–1893.

Style of dress after the fall of the crinoline—Narrow skirts—The Princesse robe—The Æsthetic Movement—The Woollen Movement—Rational dress—Changes in underclothing—Influence of modern customs on costume ... 273

CHAPTER V.

Court dress—Its contrast to fashionable dress generally—Festivities under the Regency—Abolition of hoops—Court dress in the Victorian era—Military dress ... 290

CHAPTER VI.

Changes in the costume of the commonalty—Dress of servants—Cheapening of materials—Apparel of the working classes: its unsuitability—Shams ... 305

CHAPTER VII.

Trade and commerce—The silk manufacture—Rise of alpaca—Cashmere and Paisley shawls—Lace-making—The woollen trade—Linen—Cotton—The glove trade—Pins—Jewellery—Patriotism in costume ... 310

CHAPTER VIII.

Conclusion ... 331

LIST OF ILLUSTRATIONS.

―――•>•―――

                                                                        PAGE

QUEEN VICTORIA ... ... *Frontispiece*

    This portrait shows the Queen a few years after her accession. Her Majesty wears the crown and State mantle, the Order of the Garter on the left arm, and the Order of St. George.

SIMON FRASER ... ... *To face* 16

    In the full flowing wig worn before tie-wigs and bag-wigs came into fashion.

MRS. FITZHERBERT ... ... *To face* 88

    In the most picturesque coiffure of the late eighteenth century, when regularly made "heads" were no longer worn. The ruff-like collar is a noticeable feature in this costume.

JOHN LAW ... ... *To face* 104

    In early eighteenth-century costume, with full-bottomed wig, long velvet coat heavily frogged, and embroidered waistcoat.

L. E. LANDON ... ... *To face* 212

    This portrait gives an excellent representation of the fashion which prevailed during the first quarter of the nineteenth century of dressing the hair in loops on the top of the head.

CATHERINE STEPNEY ... ... *To face* 246

    The large hat with drooping feathers, lace, flowers and ribbons resembles what were called "dress hats," which were worn at the opera and at evening parties in the early part of the nineteenth century.

THE EIGHTEENTH CENTURY.

ENGLISH DRESS.

CHAPTER I.

Transition from seventeenth to eighteenth century—Servile copying of French fashions—Similarity to the fashions of the sixteenth century.

> "He was a fool through choice, not want of wit,
> His foppery without the help of sense
> Could ne'er have risen to such excellence:
> Nature's as lame in making a true fop,
> As a philosopher; the very top
> And dignity of folly we attain
> By studious search and labour of the brain;
> By observation, counsel, and deep thought:
> God never made a coxcomb worth a groat.
> We owe that name to industry and arts,
> An em'nent fool must be a man of parts."
>
> EARL OF ROCHESTER.

THE history of the latter part of the seventeenth century is a history of retrogression, as far as social life is concerned. As the Stuart Dynasty drew to a close, costume, manners, the whole tone of society went on a downward course with break-neck speed. All that was good in the Puritan Movement, the self-restraint it imposed, the simplicity of living, the purity of thought, the stern justice of action, became mere matter for ridicule during the wild *abandon* of the Restoration. The austerity of the Puritans impelled the Royalists to greater sensuality. With the temper that prevailed in the nation at large, it was inevitable that there should be a loss of refinement in outward things accompanying the general laxity of life.

The short and troublous reign of James II. brought little change in social matters. James was very far from wishing to see reforms introduced; and though the influence of his Queen, Mary Beatrice of Modena, gave a somewhat higher stamp to the Court, she could not stem the tide of licentiousness. Dress suffered also with the decline in manners. Picturesqueness was exaggerated until it grew into grotesqueness, and the affectation of simplicity developed into artificiality. One section of society was too rigid to care for beauty, and the other too unrestrained to distinguish between luxury and extravagance, too blind to be offended by eccentricities.

In this condition of things we were ready to fall in with any new mode that presented itself, to come under the sway of any foreign influence that chanced to reign. The magnificence of the Court of Louis XIV., overcast for a time by the severe tone introduced by Madame de Maintenon, had long been the standard in England. We faithfully imitated the richness displayed under the *Grand Monarque*, and copied French fashions of dress and of entertainment. In manners we were behind: we could not follow the French in their aptitude for veiling coarseness under an appearance of refinement, and the Court, the stage, and literature were openly profligate, while the French covered their laxity with outward decorum.

But towards the close of the seventeenth century another influence made itself felt. The Stuarts were driven out, and a sovereign who cared nothing for show, a politician absorbed with great questions of international import, a stranger and a foreigner, occupied the throne. Under other circumstances a change of rulers would not have greatly affected social life, and the very brief period of William the Third's reign would not have given a different stamp to society except for the fresh influences at work. But to a period of play and masquerading had succeeded a period of earnest action. The fear of Papistry caused many a good Royalist to swerve from the falling cause of the Stuarts, and politics assumed a new importance when it became a question of deciding the succession. Gallants discussed the state of parties instead of the latest scandal, and were more concerned with Ministerial measures than with the result of their tailor's last visit to Paris. Court life was sombre, and dress and manners were equally stiff. William and Mary came with the Dutch fashions, which, superadded to the already degraded Stuart costume, gave it a quaint mixture of dignity and grotesqueness. The dress which Vandyke loved to paint was travestied, and we were ready for any new devices. As for the King, he had little interest in the matter, and cared no more about the cut of a coat or the length of a peruke than he did about the invention of a new sauce or the pattern of a tapestry hanging. William of Orange had no thoughts to spare for the whims of fashion. Rigid and conservative in social matters, he followed the customs of the country in which he had been bred. He did not favour extravagance or eccentricity in dress, but neither did he initiate reform. Queen Anne abided by tradition, and when with her accession the Eighteenth Century was ushered in, it found England, as far as costume went, in a state of degeneration.

At this juncture a period of elaboration reigned in France; we were beset with artificiality in all sorts of forms, and were without either the will or the power to free ourselves. Just as there was revulsion from stiffness and pomposity at the beginning of the previous century, so there was at its close a strange leaning towards the style which had been discarded. In women's dress, especially, there was a strong kinship between the characteristics of costume in the eighteenth and those in the sixteenth century. The intervening Stuart Period, with its careless grace, was a sharp contrast to both its predecessor and successor. It was as far removed from one as the other. Women gave up farthingales, only to jump, after an interval, into hoops ; and exchanged the elaborately curled and bejewelled coiffure of Queen Elizabeth's days for a complete structure of false hair, powder, feathers, and ribbons. The analogy might be carried out with considerable minuteness.

No period has afforded so much material for caricaturists as the eighteenth century with its multifarious fashions, its dandyism, and its feminine absurdities. "It has become by general consent an object for ridicule and sarcasm. Its very dress and airs had something about them which irresistibly moves a smile." And yet it had its graces, too. It may have been an age of " foppery and weakness, of stiletto and mask," but dress was not invariably grotesque, men were not all macaronies, and women were not all milliners' puppets. We laugh at the elaboration of toilet, at the tricks and artifices of our forefathers which history has revealed; but they, in their turn, could they speak, would be amazed at our rejection of luxury, our severe utilitarianism, and they would be scandalized by our blunt manners in society and levelling tendencies. That we are not so certain of our own wisdom is shown by the constant reversion to some bygone form, some forgotten style, to help our lame ingenuity in devising fresh fashions to appease the insatiable appetite for variety.

CHAPTER II.

The reign of the wig—How the wig came in—The wig in France—Powder—Skill of French *perruquiers*—Varieties of wigs worn in England—Lord Bolingbroke and the tie-wig—Cost of wigs—How wigs were stolen—Decline of the wig—Petition of wig-makers—The powder tax—Wigs discarded after French Revolution.

> "And now for to dress up my beau with a grace,
> Let a well-frizzled wig be set off from his face,
> With a bag quite in taste from Paris just come,
> That was made and ty'd up by Monsieur Frisson,
> With powder quite grey, then his head is complete;
> If dress'd in the fashion, no matter for wit."

THE wig is the great feature in the dress of the eighteenth century. It stands forth as the type of the character of that period, embodying the artificiality, the mixture of dignity and affectation, and the pompous conventionality which mark the last century. The wig crept in gradually. It was feeling its way in the sixteenth century under the guise of false hair. Fools and jesters wore what might be called wigs, and the fashion that then prevailed among women of frequently changing the colour of the hair suggests the idea that, instead of the troublesome and noxious process of dyeing, ladies sometimes resorted to the easier method of having different coiffures ready-made. It is asserted that Queen Elizabeth wore perukes of various colours. But, if she did, the fashion did not become general, and as far as men were concerned there was no pretence at all to anything of the sort, the hair being short and simply arranged. It was the long hair of the seventeenth century that really gave the wig its great opportunity. The elaborately curled Cavalier grew into the bewigged gentleman of the cocked hat.

The wig was worn much earlier in France. At the time when Charles I. was reigning in England, and men were still wearing their hair short, the French had already been seized with a desire for flowing locks, and their impatience caused them to adopt the *perruque*. They began to powder it, too, with white flour, but put the flour on so dry that it would not stick to the wig, and, the upper garments becoming spoilt, powder was given up for a time. What induced the French to adopt powder, and force such an inconvenient fashion upon the world, cannot be determined. Like some other modes, it is thought to have had its origin in a freak. There was a fair held, in 1614, at St.

Germain's, and some ballad singers who were performing there covered their heads with flour to make themselves look ridiculous. The lively French people, tickled with the idea, adopted it with enthusiasm, and floured heads became the rage.

Wigs then were very unnatural-looking headpieces. No one could pretend to mistake them for real hair. The first attempts at wig-making in France were very crude. But the French speedily acquired great skill, and the magnificent wigs worn by Louis XIV. were quite artistic compositions. Those were palmy days for the *barbiers-perruquiers*, as the wig-makers were called, and they became a most important trade fraternity. Every Frenchman who could afford it, and every Englishman living in France, wore a wig. Sir Ralph Verney, in the midst of his straits during his enforced residence abroad, felt himself compelled to follow the mode which at that period—1646—had not reached England. That otherwise exemplary gentleman, who acted as mentor to the whole of his large family connection, paid twelve livres for a wig when he was short of money for household necessaries. It was an elaborate wig curled in great rings, with two locks tied with black ribbon, and made without any parting at the back.

Powder, which had resumed its sway, and was no longer a simple coating of flour, was not well compounded in France. Sir Ralph writes to his wife that good hair-powder is very difficult to get. It was an appreciable addition to the weight of the wig, large quantities being used, as much as two pounds at a time occasionally. The expense must also have been considerable. Pomatum made of fat, and that sometimes rancid, was used to make the powder stick, and noxious substances were introduced into powder, as a certain kind is mentioned which must not be used alone, or it would produce headache. Our ancestors were inclined to play very freely with powerful poisons in the pursuit of beauty. Addison, in his amusing essay called *Dissection of a Beau's Head*, describes how, in one of the cavities of the skull, was found "a kind of powder which set the whole company a-sneezing, and by the scent discovered itself to be right Spanish."

The staple ingredient of powder might be flour, starch, alabaster, or plaster of Paris. There were various coloured powders, and coal dust was the foundation of common black powder. The best was not much more pleasant to use, being made of starch mixed into a paste with the blackest Japan ink and ivory black. Hair-powder was generally perfumed. There were musk, civet, ambergris, bergamot, rose, violet, almond, and orange-flower perfumes, and many more of differing qualities. The perfumes were highly desirable adjuncts to the compounds used for making powders. Perfumers became expert in colouring as well as in perfuming, and were able to produce any shade and impart any scent required. It was fashionable to change the colour of the hair when putting on mourning, and the hair was shaded to match the particular degree of mourning. Then there were washes to make the wigs curl, for " my fleece of woolly hair that now uncurls " in a smart shower had a dismal, lank appearance.

> " When suffocating mists obscure the morn,
> Let thy worst wig long us'd to storms be worn."

The fashion of wearing wigs once established in France became so universal that every peasant girl was trying to sell her hair. The cry was for hair from any head, living or dead. It was the same in England: a woman's hair might serve as her dowry. One country girl made sixty pounds by her hair, and straightway married the man of her choice, not being disposed to go empty-handed to her husband. The usual price of hair was three pounds an ounce. Dealers in hair sprang up in all quarters, and enterprising traders went far and wide in search of their commodity. Dangerous characters roamed the country-side under the guise of hair merchants, and added a new terror to social life. Only the red-haired were unable to dispose of their locks, there being a great prejudice against the colour red. When wigs first came in, the three classes of persons who are said to have at once adopted them in France were the bald, the courtesans, and the red-haired.

French wig-makers for a long time held the trade in their own hands. Their skill was undisputed, and their reputation grew every day. Englishmen and Germans were all wearing French wigs, and the fashion was so general in England that it was common to see porters and serving-men wearing the cast-off wigs of their employers. English gold was poured freely into the pockets of the *perruquiers*, for a handsome, well-made wig was essential to a gentleman of fashion. The colours were various—brown, black, grey, white, flaxen, and yellow.

> " Her hair is auburn, mine is perfect yellow :
> If that be all the difference in his love,
> I'll get me such a colour'd periwig."

Charles II. had set the fashion of black wigs. He wore a voluminous wig, flowing about the neck in one great curly mass. The famous comedian Suett had, among his splendid collection of stage wigs, a big black wig which had belonged to Charles II. Suett bought this at an auction, and reckoned it as one of his most valuable possessions. Unluckily all these wigs were destroyed in a fire which broke out at the Birmingham Theatre on August 19, 1792. In reference to this calamity, one wit wrote—

> " 'Twas sure some upstart Tory in his rigs
> Who fired poor Suett's long-tail'd race of wigs.
> Ah, cruel Tory, thus his all to take,
> Nor leave him one e'en for a hairbreadth's scape !
> Raise your subscriptions, every free-born soul ;
> Stripped of his wigs, behold a suffering Pole."

Suett published the following smart reply :—

> " Well—well may you joke, who perhaps have a wig,
> But my loss is severe tho', for all this here gig ;
> For if spouse is dispos'd or to wrangle or box,
> Alas ! what will keep her from combing my locks ?
> My fortune's too ruined, as well as renown,
> For in losing my wigs I am stripp'd to a crown." *

To imitate the real thing more closely, wigs were made with love locks or love knots. In the time of Charles II., the wig was arranged to fall on each side of the face with the ends drooping on the chest. Later on, it was drawn to the back, and the

* Daniel, *Merrie England.*

ends hung down behind. This led to a more formal style, to the tail tied top and bottom with ribbons, and the great silk bag resting on the back. The art of combing the wig gracefully in public was studied with great assiduity by the dandies, who carried their combs, in elegant cases, as they carried snuff-boxes, and combed their wigs in the theatre or any other place where they were in full view of an admiring throng.

Combing the wig was equivalent to twirling the moustache. "These Mercuries consist mostly of your smart dapper blades; though some very tall men have condescended to come into the fashion, which makes them appear to have no heads at all, or as if half the head lay hid in the bag behind it. It is an extraordinary entertainment to see the whole Mall crowded with this kind of puppets; and yet more so when, examining these childish figures, you read in their faces that they generally consist of persons from twenty-five to upwards of forty years of age. Some fops of fifty odd, made the first decays of age remarkable in them by this dress, which would be otherwise unnoticed. A jolly old friend of mine was taking an airing with me in the park the other day. 'What must be in these people's minds,' said he, 'that, in order to look gay, appear hoary, like the pictures

of old winter, when everything looks flourishing around them? The very breezes blow to refresh them, and sweep away the load of dust which would swelter them if they had not ingeniously prevented it by a cement of orange butter.' . . . As to the powderers of fifty, I must tell them that even I, who am in my grand climacterick, and have gone through the snow of so many winters, am not half so much powdered as they, and that therefore it cannot look decent in them. If we survey, from the head downwards, every part of their dress, there is not one but what is preposterous." *

The very huge wigs quite destroyed any illusion which could possibly be entertained as to the existence of a luxuriant crop of natural hair; but, nobody ever was deceived by a wig at that period, when it was treated as a separate appendage like the hat. It had not then been degraded to a mere concealment. No one was ashamed of wearing a wig. On the contrary, a person with any sense of dignity was ashamed of being so unfashionable as to wear his own hair. It was a glorious time for those to whom Nature had been niggardly. Truly, as "Dromio" says in *The Comedy of Errors*, "there's no time for a man to recover his hair that grows bald by nature," but he might

* R. Steele, *The Plain Dealer*.

"pay a fine for a peruke, and recover the lost hair of another man." Or, if not the "hair of another man," there was the horse always at hand, and his mane and tail were frequently laid under contribution.

The full flowing wig of the days of Louis XIV. was exchanged, after his time, for a wig divided into three parts, the middle piece at the back forming a *queue*, while the tresses on each side were called *cadenettes*. The queue was at first only worn by soldiers, but after the army had made it familiar it began to be adopted by civilians. Towards the end of the reign of Louis XV. the bag wig was in vogue. By this time the big flowing wigs had, for the most part, been given up in favour of what were called tie-wigs. The tie or the Ramilies wig was not at first considered quite full-dress. Queen Anne was one day greatly scandalized at Lord Bolingbroke, who had been hastily summoned, appearing before her in a tie-wig. This wig had a plaited tail, tied at the top with a large ribbon bow, and at the bottom with a smaller one. The Queen remarked that she supposed next time Lord Bolingbroke would come in his night-cap. It was the same offending nobleman who brought in the fashion of the tie-wigs. Prince Eugene of Savoy, when he visited Queen Anne, in 1712, was very much disconcerted at finding full-bottomed wigs *de rigueur* at Court. He refused to put on the unfamiliar article, and proceeded to the ante-room in the obnoxious tie-wig. Mr. Secretary St. John, who accompanied the Prince, quite eclipsed him with his long flowing wig. The Prince being told that the Queen "could not abide any one that was presented to her without a full-bottomed periwig," hurriedly sent out to his attendants to inquire if any of them possessed a wig of the approved kind, grumbling much at English etiquette. Not one of his suite, however, could help him, and he had to present himself in his tie-wig, at which Anne was greatly offended.

Besides the tie-wigs, there were the bob-wigs, minor and major. These came in during the reign of George II. The bob-wig was a direct imitation of the natural hair, and was used chiefly by the commonalty. The 'prentice minor bob was close and short; the citizen's bob major, or Sunday buckle, had several rows of curls. Every profession and almost every calling had its peculiar wig, and the oddest appellations were given to them. The caricatures of the period represent full-fledged lawyers with a towering frontlet and a long bag at the back tied in the middle; while students of the University have a wig flat on the top, to accommodate their stiff, cornered hats, and a great bag like a lawyer's at the back. The bag-wigs are said to have had their origin among the French servants, who tied up their hair in a black leather bag as a speedy way of dressing it, and to keep it out of the way, flowing curls being thought out of place for a man waiting at table. When bags were adopted by gentlemen they were made of silk, not leather. The bag-wig was not so quickly popularized in England as the other varieties. University students in the eighteenth century were very particular about their appearance, and never dined in hall without first having their wigs carefully dressed. In most of the colleges, at both Oxford and Cambridge, there were rooms set apart for the important and delicate operation of powdering. Doctors and lawyers seem generally to have worn tie and bag wigs. There were wigs for children of all ages: Queen Anne's son, the little Duke of Gloucester, wore a large white wig when he was only seven years old.

In 1760 a peruke-maker, called M. de la Papillon, and advertising himself as a pupil of the celebrated Paris artist, Sieur Latoupe, announced in the *Grand Magazine* that "he fabricates all kinds of perukes for churchmen, lawyers, physicians, military, mercantile, and country gentlemen, in a new, exquisite, curious, and extraordinary taste. As, for example, to ecclesiastical perukes he gives a certain demure, sanctified air; he confers on the tye-wigs of the law an appearance of great sagacity and deep penetration; on those of the faculty of physick he casts a solemnity and gravity that seems equal to the profoundest knowledge. His military smarts are mounted in a curious manner, quite unknown to every artist but himself. He throws into them what he calls the animating buckle, which gives the wearer a most war-like fierceness. He has likewise invented a species of Major or Brigadier for the better sort of citizens and tradesmen which, by adding a tail to them that may be taken off or put on at pleasure, may serve extremely well when they do duty in the militia. He also flatters himself upon hitting the taste of country gentlemen and fox-hunters by his short-cut bobs of nine hairs of a side. . . . For young gentlemen of the law who are not troubled with much practice, he has invented a peruke, the legs of which may be put into a smart bag during the time of vacation, and which in term time may be restored to its pristine form. . . . For such as love to save their cash, he will have perukes made of calves' tails, which he engages will last a long time. He has by long study and labour discovered and invented a commodious machine, called the night basket, by which ladies and gentlemen may have their heads dressed while they divert themselves at cards without loss of time. . . . He has an admirable secret to colour all kinds of hair on the head, and give it any tint the wearer pleases."

The cost of a handsome wig would sometimes amount to thirty, forty, and fifty guineas, though Swift grumbled at paying three guineas, and the exceedingly correct Mr. Pepys bought wigs at two and three pounds. Wigs could be had at all prices, being worn by every class of the community. It is related that there was frequently a holocaust of wigs at certain club meetings; the members finishing the revels on club nights by throwing their wigs into the fire. These were probably worn-out or cheap wigs, put on for the occasion. The scent from this bonfire of horsehair; pomatum, and powder must have been anything but pleasant.

Wigs were a great temptation to thieves, who showed surprising ingenuity in capturing their booty. They would get behind hackney coaches, which were generally compelled to go at a slow pace owing to the narrowness of the streets and the absence of proper paving, and would cut out the back and snatch a gentleman's wig from his head in a trice. The ladies lost their head-dresses in the same way. Sometimes a gentleman would find himself suddenly denuded of his head-covering in the street by an unseen hand from above, the thief being a small boy hidden in a basket, which was carried on the head of a fictitious baker. The poet Gay gives the following advice to the foot-passenger :—

> "Where the mob gathers, swiftly shoot along,
> Nor idly mingle in the noisy throng :
> Lur'd by the silver hilt, amid the swarm,
> The subtil artist will thy side disarm.
> Nor is thy flaxen wig with safety worn ;
> High on the shoulder, in a basket borne,
> Lurks the sly boy whose hand to rapine bred,
> Plucks off the curling honours of thy head."

In the latter half of the eighteenth century, during the reign of Louis XV., a great dispute arose between the wig-makers and the hair-dressers who designed coiffures. The wig-makers being a stirring, energetic body, forming one-sixth of industrial Paris, tried to monopolize the whole of the hair trade, and encroached upon what the *friseurs* considered their privilege, viz. the making of ladies' perukes, called then *chignons*. The Parliament of Aix decided in favour of the hair-dressers against the wig-makers of Marseilles; the Parliament of Paris in favour of the wig-makers against the hair-dressers of the capital. A proposal that the two bodies should amalgamate was received with indignant scorn by the hair-dressers, who thought it beneath their dignity as artists to ally themselves with mere mechanical workers like the wig-makers. A few of the more timid yielded when they found no other legitimate means of livelihood open to them, but the rest defied the mandate which had been pronounced against them, and followed their calling surreptitiously. Their position, however, became so intolerable that, after about eight years, when Louis XVI. was on the throne, the miserable *friseurs* petitioned to be allowed to practice their art on any conditions, and as a result six hundred members were added to the corporation of *barbiers-perruquiers*.

The wig-makers continued to flourish as long as Monarchy lasted, but under the Revolution they suffered so severely that many of them fled from Paris to London, where they did not probably meet with a very hearty welcome from their English fellow-workers, who were jealous of foreigners. The Master Peruke Makers of London had grown into a considerable body, with a due sense of their own interests and importance. As early as 1763 they presented a petition to King George III., complaining, among other things, of the presence of so many French hair-dressers. Their chief grievance, however, was that English gentlemen had taken to wearing their own hair. Such a fashion, the peruke-makers averred, was not only disastrous to their own trade, but ruinous to the ribbon-weavers and other persons. Curiously enough there were among the petitioners a few men without wigs. Being observed by the crowd outside St. James's Palace, they were seized and shorn of their locks, there and then, the rough, justice-loving populace having no patience with men complaining against what they themselves practised. The King listened graciously to the petitioners, and promised to do his best for them, but that was not much. As nobody wore wigs for the sake of the wig-makers, so, when it was a question of leaving them off, nobody consulted the interests of that aggrieved body. Some of the younger members of the *beau monde* took to having their own hair dressed and powdered. It was arranged in the same style as the wig.

After the Ramilies wig, which had a long run of popularity, came the Macaroni toupee with a large queue, which required the hair to be very long to be fashionable. The wig, having been made to imitate natural hair, became in its turn the model, and the natural hair was arranged to imitate the wig. As far as comfort and cleanliness went the wig was a preferable fashion, for when real hair was worn, it was smeared like the wig with pomatum, tortured with curling irons, and encrusted with more or less noxious powder.

Careful consideration had to be given to the dressing of the hair in relation to the hat. With some styles it was next to impossible to wear a hat unless the hair-dresser's pains were to go for nothing. The gentlemen, unlike the ladies, submitted to having their hair dressed every day, but the more careful ones had their curls put in papers at night to save time in the morning. The hair once dressed, a gentleman had to be cautious in his behaviour, and not let his head rub against anything; and if he were going to pay a call he avoided putting on his hat, but carried it under his arm. There was no lolling comfortably back in smoking-room lounges; every man who valued his appearance sat bolt upright. Perhaps the uncomfortable seats which furnished eighteenth-century houses owe their rigid character to the elaborate hair-dressing of both sexes, which made easy-chairs and sofas a mockery. A compromise between the wig and the natural hair was afforded by the "tower" or "half" wig, which was invented for those who were bald on the top of the head only. These "towers" came as far as the crown of the head and the back of the ears, where the real hair joined. This kind of wig was intended as a deception to give the appearance of natural hair.

When the Revolution came, an outcry arose in France against powder. The use of any farinaceous substance for mere adornment was deprecated as taking the bread out of the people's mouths. The men of the *ancien régime* still clung to the old fashion, and in the army powdered wigs were worn for a good while. In England, powder was not given up by civilians until 1795, when Pitt put a tax upon it in the hope of adding to the revenue. But the Revolution dealt a death-blow to the wearing of wigs at all, powdered or unpowdered.

For a time, of course, powder continued to be worn, and the tax was evaded by all sorts of means; but the fops grew tired of powder at length, and caused it to be tabooed, greatly to the discomfiture of hair-dressers. The tax was said to have raised in the first year £200,000, being a guinea a head for every person who used powder at all. The fine was twenty pounds for using powder without obtaining the guinea certificate. Probably the tax realized a good deal more than £200,000 a year. It was calculated that it would produce £450,000, and offers were made to farm it for £400,000. Those who used little were forced to pay as much as those who used a great deal of powder. Certain persons were exempted from paying the tax, viz. the inferior clergy, subalterns in the army, inferior naval officers, and, among private persons, all the daughters of a family but the two eldest—a very strange exception.

Party spirit entered into the wearing of powder as into other matters connected with the toilette. The Tories were the chief subscribers to the powder fund; they preferred paying the tax to giving up their powdered heads, and went by the name of "guinea pigs," while the Whigs wore their hair short, *à la guillotine*, and discarded powder. One of Gillray's caricatures of this period is entitled "Leaving off powder, or a frugal family saving a guinea." A writer in the *Gentleman's Magazine*, in 1762, proposed that a tax should be put upon perukes, except on those intended for exportation. If the idea had been adopted, what a change of fashion there would have been!

Among the epigrams which appeared on the powder-tax was the following:—

> "Full many a chance or dire mishap
> Oft'times between the lip and cup is;
> The tax that should have *hung* our *dogs*
> Excuses them and falls on puppies."

Towards the end of the reign of Louis XVI., the

natural hair was worn curled and crimped, and tied behind in a queue by those who had enough of their own to treat in this way; the political and social upheaval brought in a taste for more simplicity.

In England, too, the wig, as we have seen, fell out of favour with the younger men, and among those who still wore it there was no desire to increase its size. Even as early as 1768, the Lord Mayor of London had discarded a full-bottomed wig. Perhaps the gentlemen thought it hopeless to rival the imposing structures of the ladies, or perhaps they were tired of carrying about such a mass of hair. At any rate they made no attempt to add to the dimensions of their wigs, and before the close of the century discarded them altogether. Wigs then became part of State dress, and were afterwards relegated to the learned professions. The army retained the queue till 1808, there being an unaccountable reluctance among military men to give up what must have been to them a specially inconvenient fashion.

The clergy also retained their wigs a long time. Archbishop Tillotson, one of James the Second's prelates, was the first English clergyman to wear a wig. Whatever objection might once have been entertained against the clergy for wearing false hair was soon removed, and it was, on the contrary, thought indecorous by some persons for a priest to appear without a wig. George IV. was one of these; he was a great stickler for etiquette in dress, and the wig was to him a type of all the proprieties. He considered it monstrous that a dignitary of the Church should attempt to enter the royal presence wearing his own hair. The Bishop of London once committed this indiscretion. Lord Sidmouth, Secretary of State, barred his entry, and told the King afterwards what he had done. His Majesty cordially approved of his Minister's action, and sent a message to the unlucky Bishop that he would not suffer him to be admitted until he had cut his hair off, and was duly provided with a suitable wig.

In the legal profession the wig has held its ground to this day, in spite of reforms elsewhere. It inspires the multitude with a sense of the majesty of the law, and the learning of its expositors. Without the wig there would be less reverence for authority. "When the law lays down its full-bottom'd periwig, you will find less wisdom in bald pates than you are aware of." *

* Cumberland, *The Choleric Man.*

CHAPTER III.

Head-dresses—The "Commode"—Origin of the "Fontange"—Sudden fall of the high head-dress—Its reappearance—Art of preparing "heads"—Dispute between two *friseurs*—Hats—Various styles of coiffure—Caps—Feathers and their inconvenience—Change of style—Hair *à la Grecque*.

> "My high commode, my damask gown,
> My lac'd shoes of Spanish leather,
> A silver bodkin in my head,
> And a dancing plume of feather."
> *The Young Maid's Portion.*

REMARKABLE as was the wig, it was equalled, if not outdone, by the imposing head-dresses of the ladies. Since the fifteenth century there had been no such epoch for head-gear. The "horns" and "steeples" of the Middle Ages were scarcely more striking than the "commodes" and "heads" of the eighteenth century. Towards the end of the Stuart Period taste had begun to change. The long, careless curls were gathered up, the hair twisted and tortured into all sorts of shapes, and instead of the single flower or jewel a regular head-dress of ribbon and lace was worn. It was at the end of the reign of James II. that high head-dresses began to be seen, and when William and Mary came with the stiff, stately Dutch fashions, the coiffure of the ladies grew very erect and large. It has been described as "head-clothes." The hair was piled up high in front, and a wire frame, covered with silk and trimmed with several rows of lace and ribbons, stood on the top. From the sides of the "commode" or "tower," as this head-dress was called, hung two broad ends of lace, giving the face the shade of which it had been deprived by the loss of the curls. There were various ways of shaping this head-dress. Queen Mary wore it both broad and high; it was made of several rows of guipure point lace, with large lappets on each side. The hair beneath was fastened up in stiff curls, or rather puffs arranged horizontally. Sometimes the tiers of ribbon and lace grew very narrow at the top, and sometimes it was a sort of fan-shaped structure, widening out as it went upward.

It was not Mary, however, who was responsible for the introduction of the high head-dress. It was worn in France as well as in Holland, the forms varying in each country, and England had acquired the fashion before Mary came to the throne. The end of the seventeenth century saw

French ladies with stiff, narrow head-dresses rising straight up from the top of the head very near the forehead, the hair in closely pinned curls all round the face. The celebrated "Fontange" head-dress, which became the mode in France, arose, like many other fashions, from an accident. Mademoiselle Fontange, when out hunting with the Court one day, hastily tied up her disordered hair with a ribbon. She looked so charming in this impromptu coiffure, that her royal lover, Louis XIV., begged her to wear her hair so arranged in future; and all the Court ladies immediately followed suit. But the simplicity of this new coiffure soon became corrupted. The hair was massed in curls and puffs in a style the reverse of *negligé*, and lace was added to ribbon until a complete head-dress was created, of such an imposing size that the artistic eye of Louis was offended, and he became so disgusted with the appearance of the Court ladies that he openly expressed his disapproval.

The high head-dress came to England and flourished. It was a great deal too popular for Queen Mary's taste. Her Majesty did not at all approve of seeing City dames in head-dresses as high and important-looking as her own, even though they were not made of the best point lace. She tried to introduce a sumptuary law relating to dress, and to impose the high-crowned Dutch hat on her English subjects. This hat was similar to that which had been formerly worn by the commonalty. It greatly offended the Queen's notions of propriety to find the untitled crowd wearing gowns and head-dresses like those of great ladies. She liked to keep up distinctions in outward things, and she was frightened at the extravagance in dress which she beheld around her, and thought it a serious injury to her people's morals as well as to their pockets. But Mary, though she was greatly respected, was not a popular favourite, and the most idolized of queens would have found it almost impossible to enforce sumptuary laws at that period. The time had passed for such enactments.

In the first years of Queen Anne's reign the "tower" was still secure. Plumes of feathers added to its majesty. A fine lady, as was said, "puts on a cartload in her commode." The lace used on these commodes was a serious item. There was no imitation lace to be had then. The art of copying the exquisite productions of the Brussels and Mechlin workers was unknown in the absence of machinery. People either wore the real thing or none at all. A complete "head" of lace would cost from thirty to forty pounds of the money of that period, representing a much larger sum than now; and it must have been very trying for ladies who had bought "heads," at such a cost, when the fashion changed. This event came about in the reign of Queen Anne, who is credited with introducing the reform.

It was not France this time that brought about the change. Louis XIV. had complained in vain. The ladies of his Court refused to give up their magnificent head-dresses to please the whim of a mere man, albeit he was a king. But English ladies, for some inscrutable reason, took a dislike to their commodes, and began to dress their hair low, in a simple, graceful style. Long curls reappeared, and the front hair was combed loosely back from the face without any straining. The change was very striking. Women, who had looked taller than most of the men, were reduced to their natural stature. The French ladies were quick to follow this new fashion. What remonstrance could not accomplish, example at once effected. It was the appearance of Lady Sandwich at the French Court in a low head-dress that overthrew the towering "Fontange." To be *coiffée à l'Anglaise* became the height of fashion. Louis XIV. signified a grumbling approval, piqued that an English lady had succeeded where he had failed.

The change did not last long in England. Some

pictures represent the low coiffure as worn up to the time of George II., and depict Queen Caroline, the princesses, and ladies of the Court, with only a jewel or a flower in their hair. But the fashion veered about, for "Brussels laced heads" were certainly in vogue then. Addison relates how, within his remembrance, the head-dress went up and down "above thirty degrees." The extreme was too violent to continue: women soon tired of the low coiffure, the hoop having probably something to do with the revulsion, for there was an obvious disparity between the huge, puffed-out skirt and the flat, simply dressed hair. It made the head look ridiculously insignificant. The small caps which ladies affected about this time gave a quaintly cut-short appearance to the figure enveloped in a wide hoop. When the high head-dress once regained its place it rose more stately than ever Indeed, it grew larger when the hoop began to show signs of decline.

> "The curls which shou'd the forehead shade
> Stand staring up like horns display'd."

"Gauze heads are now the top mode," writes Mrs Delany in 1729. The gauze was a poor-looking material, and a sorry substitute for the beautiful Brussels lace. Mrs. Delany adds: "I will send you one exactly in the fashion.... You will thin it strange, coarse stuff, but it is as good as the Queen's." The ladies of George III.'s long reign wore enormous " heads," which involved so much preparation that they were often not undone for days, even weeks. On this erection, in which jewels, flowers, and ribbons all played a part, ostrich feathers a yard long were sometimes seen towering up, the feathers being placed as upright as possible to increase the height.

The curled wigs of the men shrank into insignificance beside the coiffures of the women. It was literally impossible for a lady who wore a "head" in the extreme of fashion to sit inside an ordinary hackney coach, unless she placed herself on the floor. There is a story of a lady complaining at an evening party of a pain in her shoulders caused by her having been compelled to sit with her chin resting upon her knees as she drove to the house, her head-dress being too high for the roof of the coach. Caricatures of that period represent ladies being carried in Sedan chairs with the roof open, and their head-dresses towering through the top, which, after all, was not such a gross exaggeration. Fortunately the ceilings of houses were, by the eighteenth century, tolerably lofty. The art of preparing "heads" involved the expenditure of a great deal of time and skill, and a good *friseur* could command almost any fee he demanded. The head-dress offered scope for endless ingenuity. Those who had a floral taste appeared with complete flower gardens on their heads. Others preferred fruit; others, again, ostrich feathers of various colours. Garrick did his best to ridicule these head-dresses out of existence by appearing one day on the stage dressed as a woman with a head-dress composed of all kinds of vegetables, in which carrots were particularly conspicuous. It is difficult to conceive women walking about with such a weight on their heads, much less dancing, and yet at balls the most extravagantly large erections were worn. Certainly dancing in those days was of a less lively character than now.

In France there was a great rage for feathers. They were worn in all positions on the head, and there was one particular coiffure that admitted of ten plumes. The height of the head-dresses during the reign of Louis XVI. was prodigious—for the low coiffure was only a passing fashion in France,— and the ingenuity in devising varieties of style inexhaustible. The skill of the French *friseurs* far exceeded that of ours. Indeed Archenholz described our *friseurs* as the most unskilful of any in Europe: "they perform, as in France, the office of barber and hair-dresser, and they are equally awkward at both." And another writer advises the ladies—

"Let your head-dress be modelled by Monsieur Toupee
For English friseurs can do nothing aright."

Yet we had some noted hair-dressers in England, who made fortunes, and kept their patronesses waiting for days, so much were their services in request. In France there were many female hair-dressers, but in England the only women who dressed hair were ladies'-maids, and they would not have been equal to the composition of a "head."

Nothing so altered a woman's appearance as a new style of coiffure. Horace Walpole describes his amazement at seeing a lady of his acquaintance with her head suddenly transformed. The lady had been accustomed to wear what he calls a "professed head of red hair," when one day she appeared with "no hair at all before, and at a distance above her ears I descried a smart brown bob, from beneath which had escaped some long strings of original scarlet, so like old Sarazin at two in the morning, when she had been losing at Pharaoh, and clawed her wig aside, and her old trunk is shaded with the venerable white wig of her own locks."

A lady's head-dress was infinitely more trouble

than a gentleman's wig, for besides the frizzing, the pomatum, and the powder, it had to be cunningly stuffed with pads, and false curls and *poufs* were added. A satirical writer, in 1773, observes "that it is reported that some people of fashion among the Hottentots are bidding adieu to their genteel sheepskins; for the vast quantities of warm wool that the nicest English beauties wrap their heads in to look more lovely than Venus, make them quite sick of wearing so much in waste upon their bodies." In the *Mercurius Infernus* there is a description of Don Pluto's Empress that well represents the prevailing fashion. Don Pluto finds his Empress so changed when he returned after a journey that he hardly knew her; "for she had upon her forehead a huge, monstrous, crisped and curled powdered tower," and "he observed that when she was undressing herself she not only pulled off her tower, but her whole head of hair too, and laid it in her dressing-box." The Empress probably wore a complete peruke, otherwise she would not have recklessly pulled off her "head" at night, unless it had been arranged some time and needed a new dressing. That this was not considered necessary very often may be gathered from an anecdote in *The London Magazine* for August, 1768. "I went the other morning," writes a correspondent, "to make a visit to an elderly aunt of mine, when I found her pulling off her cap, and tendering her head to the ingenious Mr. Gilchrist, who has lately obliged the public with a most excellent essay upon hair. He asked her how long it was since her head had been opened or repaired. She answered, not above nine weeks. To which he replied, that was as long as a head could well go in summer, and that therefore it was proper to deliver it now; for he confessed that it began to be a little *hazardé.*"

A noted hair-dresser, David Ritchie, who wrote a treatise on his art, naturally objected to people trying to make one dressing serve for a long time, and easily found cogent arguments against such a course. "It is certain," he wrote, "that the hair by being pinned too tight, by the movement of the head at night and the resistance of the pins, breaks or is pulled out by the roots, which may be avoided by being pinned moderately firm and frequently repeated; besides, the hair remaining long in dress, becomes matted, and contracts a dandriff at the roots which is both disagreeable and offensive." And he adds in another place, "It is very detrimental to let it remain long, without being refreshed; for the lacquer of the pins, and the powder, gathering in lumps, are apt to make it tear off in the combing out." Ritchie was valiant in the defence of powder and pomatum, and authoritatively asserts that "dressing is of great benefit to the hair; for the pomatum and powder nourish it; frizzing expands and gives it a larger body; and while it remains in dress it hath rest at the roots, which saves large quantities that would fall off by frequent combings." It is amusing to hear him complain of the English being slow in copying the more elegant fashions of the Continent. "We had," he observes, "always rejected with a kind of obstinacy any fashion which came from abroad," but had improved in that respect since the Restoration. A foreign observer remarked in noting the characteristics of social and domestic life in England, that the English "adopted the custom of dressing their hair almost against their will." There is very little trace of reluctance to follow new modes in the history of our costume, but to a skilled professor of one of the greatest mysteries of the toilet we seemed great sluggards, though impartial observers would probably say that we adopted with alacrity every fresh fashion that came in our way.

The very elaborate coiffures which were so rarely undone were confined to the fashionable world, or what quiet people called fantastical females. In the periodical literature of the day are animadversions on the "detestable and filthy fashion of wearing a load of false hair, and added to that an equal quantity of grease and powder, which, in spight of the elegant appearance of this composition of filth, cannot fail of creating some lively ideas to a squeamish stomach, which, I fear, often turns out to the disadvantage of the wearer. But yet they [these fantastical females] still persist in this enormous folly, in spight of the daily detestation which is expressed by the very men before whom they endeavour to appear amiable. Mistaken Fair! how very wide of the mark do you run! They are not to be convinced, though I am persuaded it is one of the chief causes of men's inconstancy."

In the *Court Miscellany* for 1768 is an amusing article purporting to give the history of a dispute between two fashionable *friseurs* living in Dublin —a Frenchman, M. St. Laurent, and an Italian, Signor Florentini. The Italian, discovering that the Frenchman, who by his lively conversation made himself extremely popular with ladies, was attracting most of the patronage of the city, devised a plan for undermining his formidable rival. Accordingly he issued an advertisement in the following terms: "Signor Florentini, having taken into consideration the many inconveniences which attend the method of hair-dressing formerly used by himself, and still practised by M. St. Laurent, humbly proposes to the ladies of quality in this metropolis his new method of stuccowing the hair in the most fashionable taste, to last with very little repair during the whole session of Parliament. Price only five guineas. N.B. He takes but one hour to build the head, and two for baking it."

This was answered by the Frenchman with a note of defiance. Florentini, who employed some one to compose his advertisements, which accounts for their correct phrasing, replied by pointing out with great plainness of language the inconveniences attending the method of M. St. Laurent. Among other things, "he begs to observe that three rows of iron pins thrust into the skull will not fail to cause a constant itching, a sensation that much distorts the features of the face, and disables it so that a lady by degrees may lose the use of her face; besides the immense quantity of pomatum and powder, laid on for a genteel dressing, will, after a week or two, breed *mites*, a circumstance very disagreeable to gentlemen who do not love cheese, and also does afford a fœtid smell, not to be endured." M. St. Laurent rose to the occasion, and in his imperfect English poured forth a torrent of sarcasm, wrath, and ridicule, on his traducer. "Hah! hah!

hah!" he begins, "dere is no objeshon den to Signior Florentini's vay of frizing de hair of fine ladie? I shall tell him von, two, three: in de forst place, he no consider, dat his stuccow vill be crack, and be break by the frequent jolts to vich all ladies are so sobject, and dat two hours' baking vil spoil de complekshon and hort de eyes. And as to his candeleuse aspersion dat my method breed a de *mite* so odious to gentlemen who do not love de cheese, I say 'tis false and malitieuse; and to make good vat I say, I do envite all gentlemen of qualitie to examine de hede of de Countess of —— (vich I had de honour to dress four weeks ago) next Monday at twelve o'clock, through Monsieur Closent's great mikroscope, and see if dere be any mite dere, or oder thing like de mite vateor. N.B. Any gentleman may smell her ladyship's hede sen he please."

The question naturally arises: would the Countess —— be willing to undergo a public examination, and sit to have her head *smelt* by gentlemen of quality, even to save the reputation of her favourite *friseur*? History telleth not. But whether the test was carried out or not is immaterial to the main issue, as the matter ended in a duel in which, happily, both combatants satisfied their honour without receiving injury.

The hats worn over these elaborately dressed heads were portentous. They were generally placed rather backward so as to show the mass of frizzed hair in front. How were they fastened on? They look extremely unsteady in the pictures, perched on the top of the coiffure, and as if the least breath of wind or the slightest movement would send them over. Certainly the homely but secure elastic which modern hair-dressing has forced us to relinquish was not in vogue then. Probably the hats were attached to the hair by some of those pins which the hair-dressers used in building heads. There must have been some method of uniting the hat to the wearer, though they look far enough apart with the mass of hair between.

Hats at that time seemed to have less connection with the head than at any other period. They were really unnecessary adjuncts; and the gentlemen, as we have seen, often thought so, and carried instead of wearing their hats. But ladies could not do this; custom prescribed that their hats should be on their heads—not on the real head, but on that built by the *friseur*. Eighteenth-century ladies were not particularly fond of walking exercise, certainly; they generally paid their visits and went shopping in chairs and coaches—when they could afford it. But still they liked promenading, or what they called "taking the air," in the park, and showing off their finery at Ranelagh and Vauxhall Gardens; and hats that would not keep their equilibrium except under conditions of absolute rest would be, in the phraseology of the period, "mightily" inconvenient. The *élégantes* who had spent all the morning over their toilet would never have run the risk of losing their head-gear and their dignity together in making a curtsey, for example, which must inevitably have happened unless those wonderful hats had been very firmly affixed. If it is embarrassing in the present day for a lady to have to chase her hat along a London thoroughfare, it was infinitely more so in the last century, when costume was so ill-adapted for rapid motion. The idea of any one running in a great hooped petticoat is preposterous.

Some hats were turban-shaped, with the trimming chiefly in the centre of the crown; others were low-crowned, with very wide brims turned up with a spray of flowers or over a *pouf*. Many of them had long ribbon ends hanging from the back. The hat, of course, varied with the style of hair, and this changed from one decade to another, and even from year to year. With the commode, hats could not be worn at all. Then, in the earlier part of the century, there was the smooth toupee, which consisted of stiff curls disposed lengthwise and crossways on the top of the head, while down the sides thick lumpy-looking rolls were pinned in a variety of positions. There was a special style for riding, and one astute hair-dresser advises the use of artificial curls, as no natural hair could be expected to curl "so strong as to endure the great fatigue of riding." When the rage for cabriolets or one-horse chaises came in, great caps with sides to imitate the wheels of chaises were worn. This was in 1755. The cabriolet head-dress had a host of satirists: there were head-dresses to imitate post-chaises, chairmen, and broad-wheeled waggons among the caricatures, which were produced in abundance. "Put my post-chaise upon my head," orders a fashionable lady to her maid; and the maid answers, "Your chair and chairmen, ma'am, is brought," and, a few minutes later, "And, ma'am, the milliner is come. She's brought the broad-wheeled waggon home."*

A popular cap worn in 1762 was the fly-cap, in shape like a big butterfly. It was edged with garnets and brilliants, and made a very lustrous setting for the face.

There was an odd fashion in vogue at one time

* T. Wright, *Caricature History of the Georges.*

of wearing what were called hat brims, which are described as hats without any crown. These brims were only suitable for fine, sunny weather, being nothing more than a slight shade for the eyes. At a time when hair-dressing was so elaborate, a *whole* hat was certainly superfluous and decidedly in the way. A brim was all that was needed.

In 1765 the Duchess of Bedford introduced the great "calash," an enormous round cap stiffened with whalebone. It could be drawn over the face, or thrown back, being tied under the chin. When drawn forward it looked like a barrel.

The smooth, lofty toupee was the ugliest form of coiffure that could possibly have been invented, and the one that lent itself most readily to caricature. But the reality was so extravagant it did not need exaggeration to make it appear ridiculous. The front view of a lady's head was certainly an awe-inspiring spectacle; but the back view was truly terrible, with the long straight sweep from the nape of the neck to, not the crown of the head, but the crown of the head-dress, which suggested some hideous abortion of intellect. This head-dress was complete in itself, and did not admit of a hat. Beside these smooth, towering heads, the puffed and frizzled coiffures, in which the face looked like a bird peeping out of a furze bush, were models of beauty. Extravagantly large as they were, they had at least the merit of giving shade and softness to the face, and hid the defects of badly shaped heads which the towering style accentuated.

The wide style of dressing the hair was generally accompanied by a head-dress, cap, or hat, of moderate height. At one time there was a fancy among fashionable people in London for imitating the flat straw hats worn by country lasses. There is a humorous story of a lady who was so much taken with the appearance of a milkmaid in a flat straw hat, that she immediately set to work to devise a similar head-gear for herself, and even sat for a couple of hours with two weighty volumes on her head to insure the top acquiring the desired flatness.

Grosley, writing in the early part of the reign of George III., says, "At the trial of Lord Byron, I saw only a few ladies dressed in the French taste. All the rest, decked in the finest manner with brocades, diamonds, and lace, had no other head dress but a ribband tied to their hair, over which they wore a flat hat adorned with a variety o ornaments. It requires much observation to be able to give a full account of the great effec produced by this hat. It affords the ladies wh wear it that arch roguish air which the winged ha gives to Mercury; it animates their faces with a degree of vivacity which is not natural to them. In the midst of these hats which filled Westminster Hall the heads of those ladies who were dressed according to the French fashion resembled unfurnished houses. No rouge was laid upon their faces; the rouge, which the Frenchwomen have doubtless borrowed from the ancient Picts, has not as yet crossed the seas." Rouge was probably never so much used here as in France, owing to the superiority of the English complexion, but it had certainly "crossed the seas" long before Grosley came to England.

The close caps, ridiculed as night-caps, worn by ladies in 1773, are described by contemporary observers as odious and frightful. If the ladies could see themselves, says one writer, "thus hoodwinked in a proper light, they would immediately throw off the disguise, and carry what is far more becoming — an open countenance. Were these favourite caps enjoined by an Act of Parliament, it would be deemed as great a grievance as the Middlesex election, and I doubt not they would be ready enough to comply with the fashion of the times, and petition for a redress." The use of the term "hood-winked" gives some idea of the shape of these caps; and the close caps made with wings, which are given as the correct undress for February of that year, were no doubt the offending articles. The style of hair varied constantly, and in France there were complaints that the ladies were trying to copy the gentlemen by wearing their hair in a catogan in imitation of the queue. In this same year, 1773, a lady in London might wear her hair in three different ways, and be equally fashionable in them all. She might wear a "slope bag with no curls, the front toupee brought high and straight," or "a long bag with about six long curls," or "the hair straight, with about nine curls crossways."* These fashions were for the first month of the year. By the autumn, hair was worn low in front, and high at the back, for full dress; and, for undress, in curls, and flat on the top. Small chip hats went with this style of hair-dressing.

Throughout the year 1775 the manner of dressing the hair was very unbecoming. It was rolled up tightly in front, rather high, and drawn severely away from the face, while at the back were numerous stiff-looking rolls, called curls, pinned close to the head, with two "drop curls" of the sausage type on each side, just below the ears. For full dress, three large ostrich feathers would be placed at the very top of the head, rather near the front, or a

* *The Lady's Magazine.*

worked head-dress was worn, made quite flat on the top, and having large lace lappets, which projected rather than fell over the sides of the face. The fashions were not improved in the following year. The hair was still dragged up from the front and back, and surmounted either by the winged cap or a turban.

By 1780 we find a more tasteful style prevailing. Instead of the hair being dragged away from the face, it was allowed to droop a little over the forehead in small curls, and was either coiled or plaited at the back. Curls at the side relieved the stiffness of what was still an elaborate style. The next year sees the hair still low on the top, with curls falling about the forehead and neck, and small hats in vogue. In this year fashion decreed suddenly that for full dress no cap and no ornaments should be worn, the hair being braided with pearls and ribbon. For undress, however, the winged cap was still in use. At the King's birthday celebration in 1786 the princesses wore their hair dressed in the wide style. The head-dress of the Princess Royal was not at all high. The black feathers which she wore drooped at the back, and the lappets of lace, with a spray of flowers in the centre, fell from the low crown, which was encircled by a cord of diamonds. The ladies present at the festivities are described as having their heads dressed very wide, in curls, and wearing caps made of crape—a favourite material for dresses also—with flowers and plumes for trimming.

The French head-dresses at this period were very large indeed, and the hair was worn in a wide frizzed mass all round the head, with long curls peeping out under a big cap-bonnet, more like a monstrous mob, with an enormous ribbon bow at one side. In England some pretty, broad-brimmed hats were worn over these frizzed coiffures, large black chips very simply trimmed, and picturesque Rubens hats of black velvet, turned up near the front, with white feathers. There was also a new head-dress, called the Terque, something like an hussar's cap, covering the front of the hair. It was made of ribbons, with a plume of feathers in the middle, and another large plume at the back; but it was so unbecoming that few people adopted it. During the year 1786, the hair was sometimes dressed quite low in the front, and sometimes high, but generally projecting at the sides. The *chignon*—not a round lump, but an elaborate arrangement of coils—was worn low. In France the word was used for a complete peruke. "Les perruques de femmes," says M. Quicherat, "s'appelèrent des chignons;" but in England it was restricted to the back portion of the hair. For semi-dress, powder might be dispensed with, but the hair must always be curled in some form or other. When what was called the Pantheon cap came in, the hair was specially arranged for this head-gear in very large curls, all massed in the front. The cap, composed of blond, flowers, and feathers, was round and small, and placed rather backward, with a large filmy veil hanging down behind.

Some fashions had queer origins. For instance, there was the cap called the Ranelagh mob, because it was so much seen in those celebrated gardens. It was made of gauze, twisted about the head, crossed under the chin, and fastened behind with the ends hanging down. Some of the market women, who sold green stuff in Covent Garden, used to wear silk handkerchiefs wrapped round their heads in this way; and a certain lady of not very reputable character took a fancy to this head-gear, and made herself a mob like it in fine lawn. Others followed her example, and the women of the town who appeared at Ranelagh in these mobs set the fashion to the polite world.

A large cap was always worn for undress, especially the cap with wide wings. Hoods made of blond and crape turbans were thought very elegant head-dresses. Both young and old always wore some kind of cap or head-dress in the house. There was plenty of variety in outdoor headgear—large bonnets, small hats, caps and hoods to suit all faces. Coloured hoods edged with fur were very becoming; and pretty combinations were made, such as pink, trimmed with ermine. Politics affected headgear like other parts of dress; and the ladies who espoused the cause of Charles James Fox, when that statesman was in the zenith of his fame, wore a fox's tail in their bonnets. It is very odd to find black lace bonnets with a cape or curtain at the back, worn over a hood made of white lawn tied under the chin. This fashion survived in the bonnets with white frilled fronts, that used to be worn many years ago, and may still be seen among old-fashioned country folk.

Then there was the "Devonshire hat," named after the famous beauty. This hat was made of chip straw and trimmed with white feathers. It was particularly specified that no cap was to be worn with this hat. At the time when the beautiful Duchess was the reigning belle, caps began to be discarded. An improved style of hair-dressing came in; the ugly lump called the "false chignon" being abolished, and long, powdered curls of the natural hair falling on the shoulders. The lofty head-gear, however, did not go out all at once. In 1791 its inconvenience in public places was still so much felt that when the music meetings were taking place in Westminster Abbey it was ordered that no one wearing a cap of a larger size than the pattern exhibited in the Lord Chamberlain's office should be admitted. Many ladies who wished to attend these performances found it impossible to get their heads dressed early enough in the morning, the hair-dressers being all so busy, and went through this part of their toilet the night before, taking infinite pains to sleep in such a position that the dressing might not be disarranged.

Up to 1792 the Parisian ladies wore their hair very elaborately frizzed and curled, and their head-dresses were extremely large; but in the autumn of that year came a decided change. There was no more curling and frizzing, no piling up of great knots of hair, and the fashion journals expressed a hope that the world had seen the last of the enormous head-dresses. In England, several leaders of fashion, in the same year, put their veto on the large heads; notably, the Duchess of Rutland, Lady Anne Fitzroy, and Lady Molineux. The royal princesses, especially the younger ones, seem to have worn their hair in a loose, curly mass, which may, however, have been an arrangement of the painter. Pictures cannot always be trusted to represent fashions faithfully in the eighteenth century; for the painters, like those of the present day, often tried to improve on the prevailing modes, which they found too stiff and inartistic for their brushes. They liked to idealize the accessories. When they were anxious to produce an attractive portrait they took some pardonable liberties with the costume of the sitter. Kneller, says Walpole, " had exaggerated the curls of full-bottomed wigs and the tiaras of ribands, lace, and hair, till he had struck out a graceful kind of unnatural grandeur; but the succeeding modes were still less favourable to picturesque imagination. The habits of the time were shrunk to awkward coats and waistcoats for the men, and, for the women, to tight-laced gowns, round hoops, and half a dozen squeezed plaits of linen, to which dangled behind two unmeaning pendants called lappets, not half covering the straight-down hair." *

But hair was certainly much simpler and prettier, and occasionally the head-dresses worn at Court, even on royal birthdays, were very moderate, sometimes consisting only of a bandeau of diamonds and a few feathers, though the turban-shaped caps of black and coloured velvet were very much in use for Court costume. At the royal

* *Anecdotes of Painting in England.*

birthday festivities in June, 1795, a chronicler notes that hardly a cap was to be seen. There was nothing worn but bandeaux. Here may be noted the influence of the classic style which dominated at this period. The English, like the French, modelled their dress on that of the ancient Greeks, or, rather, attempted to do so, and bound their hair with fillets in imitation of the Greek women. Sometimes these bands were of muslin, and narrow strips of coloured embroidery were also frequently used. The hair was dressed quite close to the head, instead of standing out from it, as had been the fashion, and the short, curly mass over the front looks very modern. The coiffure was arranged to harmonize with the simple, hoopless gowns which came in at this time.

But though the style of the hair was so much prettier and more graceful, it was by no means simple, and false hair was largely used. A fashionable hair-dresser in Bond Street advertised, in 1795, that he had a stock of chignons or braids in eight lengths, from ten shillings to six guineas each. "Brunswick fillets," which were thought something super-elegant, were sold "with curls complete, fit either for morning or full dress, from seven and sixpence to ten and sixpence each." This obliging hair-dresser notified his willingness to change chignons that were not approved, if they had not been powdered. That there were many who still clung to towering head-gear is shown by a satirical paragraph which appeared in the *Times*, in 1794, declaring that ladies wore feathers exactly of their own length, so that a woman of fashion was twice as long upon her feet as in her bed. The same paper, which, at that period, delighted in ridiculing the fashions, announced that "at all elegant assemblies there is a room set apart for the lady visitants to put their feathers on, as it is impossible to wear them in any carriage with a top to it. The lustres are also removed upon this account, and the doors are carried up to the height of the ceiling. A well-dressed lady who nods with dexterity can give a friend a little tap upon the shoulder across the room without incommoding the dancers. The ladies' feathers are now generally carried in the sword-case at the back of the carriage." A little later came a paragraph as follows: "There is to be seen in Great Queen Street a coach upon a new construction. The ladies sit in this well, and see between the spokes of the wheels. With this contrivance the fair proprietor is able to go quite dressed to her visits, her feathers being only a yard and a half high."

For outdoor wear there were all sorts of bonnets

and hats, but no more hoods among fashionable people. Lace veils were worn to the bonnets in 1789, and a writer to the *Lady's Magazine* bemoans this fashion, which concealed the face. " Dear Ladies!" he writes, "have pity on us; and be assured that one peep at your fair faces is worth all the Brussels lace, notwithstanding the cobweb texture, that ever was imported." There were also bewitching-looking straw hats with open brims, tied under the chin, worn in summer, and straw hats so close and round as to look like caps, with which dainty little white veils were worn halfway over the face, as used to be the fashion a few years ago. In winter the bonnets, which were generally of velvet and very closely fitting, were edged with fur to match the tippet and muff. The rapid change of fashion in regard to head-gear gave rise to the following squib in 1796 : "Since the invention of the *Coiffure télégraphique* it is scarcely possible to follow the rapidity of fashions. The morning and the evening dress mean literally the dress of the day they are worn in. It was observed with concern, at Drury Lane, the other evening, that the Lady P——'s were more than half an hour out of fashion."

Just as the body was freed from the cumbrous hoop, so the head was freed from the ridiculous excrescences which had been piled upon it in every conceivable form. Fashion had done her worst with regard to the head. She could go no further, and the rebound was complete. The extravagant modes of the eighteenth century died out without a chance of revival. Hair-dressers never again enjoyed such halcyon days. There was no more building of "heads," no more perfumed hair-powder to be sold, and hair-dressing became, as a lawyer said of a case that would not lengthen out in spite of all his efforts, "disgustingly simple," in the opinion of the despondent *friseur*. He had his day, and it was a long one. Let him be "contented with what he has done," for he "stands but small chance of becoming famous for what he will do. He has laid down to die. The grass is already growing over him."

CHAPTER IV.

LADIES' DRESS.

The hoop—Its origin—French ladies and their hoops—Inconvenience of hoops in London streets—General fashion of dress—How we procured Parisian fashions—Patching and face-painting—How a lady lost her eyebrows—Narrow "shapes" and tight lacing—The polonaise and sacque—The fan and its uses—The muff—Sudden change of fashion—Clinging gowns—Popularity of muslins—Dress modelled on classic costume—Mixture of styles.

> " The spacious petticoat, in bright array,
> Like a tall ship does all its pride display,
> Swells with full gales, and sweeps along the way."
> JOSEPH GAY, *The Petticoat*.

THE distinguishing characteristic of women's dress in the eighteenth century was the hoop. It came in at the beginning, and went out, reluctantly, at the close. Not until the change of taste, which took place both in England and France after the Revolution of 1789, did the hoop lose its sway, and even then it lingered on as part of Court dress long after it had been discarded for general wear. No fashion so marked enjoyed a longer popularity.

The hoop came in disguised under the name of panier. It was in this form that it insinuated its unwieldy bulk into the gowns, and, having secured admittance, quickly grew too large and strong to be expelled. Where the panier came from nobody knows. Certainly not from France, for the French took it from us. M. Quicherat ingeniously suggests that the old wheel farthingale had survived in some little German Court, and was thence re-imported to England as the panier. This, however, does not explain who brought it. We only know that it came, and that it stayed. The looping up of the gown into the form of the panier began at the close of the seventeenth century, and was the first intimation of the new style which was to continue for nearly a hundred years. We have had many revivals since of the bunched-up skirt, and it is always accompanied by much trimming. So it was then. Frills were introduced, and frills mean gowns of an indifferent cut. The natural lines of the figure were destroyed by the expansion of the hips. Taste had swung right round; the flowing style was out of favour, and the panier speedily turned into the hoop-petticoat.

In France it was called at first *panier-à-coude*, because it served as an elbow-rest. It was very much like the old wheel farthingale in form. The

French, who from being our teachers, were now to become our imitators, hesitated a little before encumbering themselves with this new burden; but, once adopted, the hoop thrived exceedingly. How enormous it became may be judged from the fact that in 1728 it was the subject of serious consideration with the Minister, Cardinal Fleury. When the Queen attended the opera she was accustomed to sit between the two princesses, and the result was that her Majesty was completely hidden by the hoops of her companions. In French eyes this amounted to a positive scandal, but it was impossible that the Queen should go to the opera unattended, and it was equally out of the question for the princesses to go without their hoops. What was to be done? Only one thing: a space must be cleared about the Queen. Orders were accordingly given that a *fauteuil* should be left vacant on either side of the Queen. This instruction was carried out, but the princesses had no intention of being eclipsed in their turn, and demanded that a similar space should be left between them and the duchesses.

It is related that a French lady, who went to confession in a hoop, was quite unable to squeeze herself through the door of the confessional and approach the grating. After repeated struggles she was obliged to give up the attempt, and return home with her load of unconfessed faults.

The hoop grew apace in England. It was so big in Queen Anne's reign, viz. between 1702 and 1714, that one would have thought it must really have finished growing. Much satire was aroused by the appearance of hoops in church. "Several congregations of the best fashion," says the *Spectator*, "find themselves already very much straitened, and if the mode increase, I wish it may not drive many ordinary women into meetings and conventicles. Should our sex at the same time take it into their heads to wear trunk breeches (as who knows what their indignation at this female treatment may drive them to?) a man and his wife would fill a whole pew."

Hoops were very much in the way when walking in the street. In the last century London, though both its business and its population were so much smaller than at present, was equally, if not more unsuited to pedestrians in distended garments. Trade was largely carried on by means of stalls, which were propped up by poles, and were easily knocked down by an unwary passer-by. The *Female Spectator* advises ladies either to leave their hoops at home, or to take a sedan chair or a coach if they wish to go out on Mondays and Fridays, in the morning, which was a specially busy time. On one occasion "a lady came tripping by with one of those mischief-making hoops, which spread itself from the steps of my door quite to the posts placed to keep off the coaches and carts; a large flock of sheep were that instant driving to the slaughter-house, and an old ram who was the foremost, being put out of his way by some accident, ran full butt into the footway, where his horns were immediately entangled in the hoop of this fine lady, as she was holding it up on one side, as the genteel fashion is, and indeed the make of it requires. In her fright she let it fall down, which still the more encumbered him, as it fixed upon his neck; she attempted to run, he to disengage himself, which neither being able to do, she shrieked, he ba'ad, the rest of the sheep echoed the cry, and the dog who followed the flock barked, so that altogether made a most hideous sound. Down fell the lady, unable to sustain the forcible efforts the ram made to obtain his liberty. A crowd of mobs, who were gathered in an instant, shouted. At last the driver, who was at a good distance behind, came up, and assisted in setting free his beast, and raising the lady; but never was finery so demolished. The late rains had made the place so excessive dirty that her gown and petticoat, which before were yellow, the colour so much revered in Hanover, and so much the mode in England at present, were now most barbarously painted with a filthy brown; her gauze cap half off her head in the scuffle; and her *tête de mutton* hanging down on one shoulder. The rude populace, instead of pitying, insulted her misfortune, and continued their shouts till she got into a chair and was out of sight."

To squeeze a lady in a large hoop into the limited space afforded by a sedan chair was not always an easy matter, and the alternative to the sedan—the hackney coach—was not much better adapted to the accommodation of hoops. Sometimes the lady found—

> "Yet found too late,
> The Petticoat too wide, the door too strait;
> Entrance by force she oft attempts to gain,
> Betty's assistance, too, she calls in vain,
> The stubborn whalebone bears her back again.
> Vex'd at the balk, on foot she trips her way,
> For woman's will admits of no delay;
> On either side a faithful slave attends,
> And safe from harm the Petticoat defends." *

Hoops were worn everywhere, at all times and seasons, in the morning as well as at the evening rout, and by young and old alike. The hoop was not like its successor, the crinoline, an under garment—if such an excrescence can be called a

* Joseph Gay, *The Petticoat.*

garment at all,—it was the outside petticoat itself, very wide, and stiffened with whalebone.

> "The whalebones spread the swelling canvas wide,
> And stretch'd their stubborn lengths from side to side."

The hoop, said its advocates, kept the wearer cool in summer; but, on the other hand, it let in the cold airs of winter. "I have heard some great ladies lately complain of terrible colds they have caught through the too great concavity of their petticoats, which they seem to dread may end in rheumatisms or seyatica's; if so, perhaps, the rest of the sex may be sooner reclaimed by their sad example, than by all your excellent precepts; but if you still find that they retain a fondness for this favourable fashion, pray desire them at least to have more regard to our domestic trade than to that of Greenland, and, in lieu of whalebone, to suffer themselves to be encompassed in wooden hoops. We make here in England of three sorts, white hoops, rind hoops, and smart hoops, so that they may all be fitted to their own liking; but I believe the latter sort will best suit with the generality of the sex, who being sensible that they are but weak vessels, and too apt to be leaky, shew their judgment in desiring to be kept well and tightly hoop'd, which, if performed with the materials above mentioned, may prove of no small benefit to the nation in general, and, by enhancing the price of timber, raise the yearly income of the estates of the fathers, husbands, or brothers of such females as shall most endeavour to extend so useful a mode; which, in a little time, may bring a plantation of hops, besides the manifest encouragement it will give to all artificers in this sort of ware." *

An amusing defence of the hoop was published in 1711 by the *Spectator*, which found much food for mirth and good-humoured sarcasm in the fashions of the day. The writer, who signs himself with the fanciful name of "Tontiloff," relates how he was walking in Kensington Gardens with a young lady who had left off her hoop in accordance with the advice of "Mr. Spectator." "To my great vexation of spirit," writes the gentleman, "I found the whole company were ridiculing and remarking this lady. Some (that did not know her) said, 'I wonder that gentleman should bring a lady of pleasure into these walks;' others said, she was mighty pretty, but it was pity she was a prude, else she would be the toast of the town: those that had the honour to know her were pleased to say they admired that lady had left off her hoop, since it made her appear with that majestic air which bespoke her something more than woman.

* *Letters to the Tatler and Spectator*, 1725.

Finding the company's thoughts so exactly agreeing with my own, I persuaded the lady to the putting it on again, that she might prevent being taken for either a prude or a coquette, they being both equally obnoxious." After a few more remarks the writer concludes, " I beg you will shortly give this a place in your speculations, for the justification of the ladies that shall re-assume the dress, and for the information of those that are ignorant of the beauty of them." *

The form of dress consisted of a petticoat, or, as it would be called now, a skirt, distended by whalebone, and called a hoop-petticoat, and a gown opening in the front, with or without a long train. The bodice of the gown was either laced up the front over a stomacher, or else smart-looking stays were worn outside, those articles being made for show, and not then relegated to the rank of underclothes. One continually meets with mention of stays in descriptions of full-dress costume. They were more like a deep, pointed waistband, with straps at the shoulders. In 1734 stays were worn extremely low, and in 1795 a paragraph in the *Times* declared, in a satirical comment on the fashions, that "corsettes about six inches long, and a slight buffon tucker of two inches high, are now the only

* *Original and Genuine Letters to the Tatler and Spectator.*

defensive paraphernalia of our fashionable belles between the necklace and the apron strings." The high stays were very ugly, and produced an unnatural-looking figure, especially as they were generally very tight. Girls were taught to hold themselves in stiff attitudes, and to prevent them from stooping a long needle was sometimes placed in front of the dress on the left side of the neck of the gown.

Damask was a favourite material for petticoats, and a damask hoop with gold and silver embroidery and fringe, such as was worn by fashionable women for full dress, cost twelve pounds or more. Velvet petticoats and "wrought" petticoats, petticoats of cloth, of silk, of chintz, of Holland embroidered in coloured silks, were also worn. We even read of ermine petticoats worn under a velvet gown trimmed with fur — a truly regal costume. Startlingly bright were the colours used, and the style of dress permitted of the use of several colours at a time. The petticoat would be of one colour, the embroidery on it of another, the gown of a third, the stays of a fourth, the apron of a fifth, the cloak of a sixth, and the hood—when such an article was worn in the absence of the commode—of a seventh.

> " The ladies, gayly dress'd, the Mall adorn
> With various dyes and paint the sunny morn."

Picture a lady of Queen Anne's days in "a black silk petticoat with a red and white calico border, cherry-coloured stays trimmed with blue and silver, a red and dove-coloured damask gown flowered with large trees, a yellow satin apron trimmed with white Persian, and muslin head-cloths with crow-foot edging, double ruffles with fine edging, a black silk furbelowed scarf and a spotted hood." As long as the commode lasted any additional head-gear was out of the question, but, when this was given up, very pretty coloured hoods were worn out-of-doors. There was at one time, during Queen Anne's reign, a fashion of wearing scarlet cloaks with the coloured hoods, which must have given the streets and public places a very gay appearance. Besides the hoods there were hats of black and white beaver, though the broad-brimmed beaver hat rather belonged to the dress of the commonalty. For a while fashionable ladies took to high-crowned hats, and a little later wore gipsy hats and small bonnets with strings tied in front, which look very much like modern bonnets.

All the gowns were made with elbow sleeves, not puffed, but rather full, and finished off with a deep frilling of muslin or lace, or else a separate muslin sleeve was worn underneath, and corresponded with the white tucker round the neck of the gown. Aprons were for ornament, not use, and were often made of the most expensive lace. The fashion of the pointed bodice and full sleeves continued practically unchanged until the last quarter of the century. Trains were not invariably worn; the hoop petticoat always cleared the ground, and was sometimes derided for being too short. One critic declared that the ladies wore their petticoats up to their knees. But trains were worn more generally as the century advanced, and worn in the public promenades and gardens, sweeping the ground. "As a lady's quality or fashion was once determined here by the circumference of her hoop, both are now measured by the length of her tail. Women of moderate fortunes are contented with tails moderately long; but ladies of true taste and distinction set no bounds to their ambition in this particular. I am told the Lady Mayoress, on days of ceremony, carries one longer than a belwether of Bantam, whose tail, you know, is trundled along in a wheelbarrow."*

It was an expensive fashion, very profitable to the silk mercers. "Nothing can be better calculated to increase the price of silk than the present manner of dressing. A lady's train is not bought but at some expense, and after it has swept

* Goldsmith, *Citizen of the World.*

the public walks for a very few evenings is fit to be worn no longer, more silk must be bought in order to repair the breach, and some ladies of peculiar economy are thus found to patch up their tails eight or ten times, in a season." The train came in a long Watteau-like pleat from the neck, but it was wider and more voluminous than the trains of the Watteau dresses of modern times.

For full dress the neck of the gown was cut low both back and front, but for ordinary wear it was sometimes high at the back and square in the front, as the gowns used to be cut for evening wear, especially for young girls, between twenty and thirty years ago. Whatever the hour or the weather nobody thought of completely covering up the neck. "Mr. Spectator" is again to the fore on this point, and publishes a letter in which a young lady is made to complain of the cold she is compelled to endure by being forced by her aunt, with whom she lives, to comply with the fashion of uncovered necks out-of-doors. All the protection she has is a scarf of some thin stuff, or, as the letter describes, "about as thick as a spider's web, and pinned down to my mantua-gown, which is no higher than the middle of my back." This young lady, belonging to a fashionable circle, wore her gown low back and front at all times. With difficulty she obtains permission to put on a handkerchief in addition, but it was not to be placed higher than the neck of the gown, and was therefore of no use.

The appearance of a lady on horseback in a fashionable London riding-habit, and tricked out in the newest guise with patches, is amusingly described by Steele. The lady is supposed to be riding through the town of Kettering in Northamptonshire, in the month of July, 1724. " Yesterday a strange and surprising creature was seen to pass through our town on horseback. It had the face of a young woman, stuck full of patches; a perriwig which hung down to its waist; a hat cock'd with the smartness of a young officer; a huge bunch of ribbons fastened behind its left shoulder; a shirt laid in large pleights on the breasts and tied close at the neck and wrists, which, with a vest of white satteen, trimmed with black, had much the resemblance of a shroud. Our whole town was soon alarmed with this strange appearance, and various are still the opinions what it really was. The old people, who were the most couragious generally, went pretty near to it with their spectacles on to view it more distinctly; the younger sort kept it at an awful distance. Some were of opinion that it was a highwayman in disguise, and accordingly were for seizing it; others took it for a nun; but by a certain arch leer it had with its eyes I dare engage it had not a bit of nun's flesh about it. However, by its pale complexion and shroud-like dress, most of my neighbours at last concluded it to be a ghost, and so took to their heels, and left me (who am no great believer in these things) almost alone with it in the road. I had now an opportunity, during the time it was drinking a glass of Rhenish wine and sugar at the Saracen's Head Inn, to survey it well, and thereupon concluding it to be an Hermaphrodite, I enquired of the man who seemed to have the keeping of it, if he intended to show it in our town, and at what inn? For you must know, Sir, that I have a mighty curiosity to see one of those creatures all over. But the man with an angry countenance told me: That what I took for an Hermaphrodite was only a young lady, and that the sort of dress she was in was commonly worn for a riding-habit by the ladies of fashion at London. But as neither I nor my neighbours can believe it possible for folks upon no ill design to disguise themselves in such a manner, I desire you will, in one of your *Plain Dealers* (for we have it constantly brought us by our coach), inform us of the truth, which will tend very much to the satisfaction of the best part of our town who are your readers. . . .

"P.S.—Since I writ my letter some of my neighbours tell me they believe the creature I have writ to you about is one of the masqueraders we have heard of that are common with you at London, but for my part I can't think it ugly enough for one of them neither." *

French fashions were exclusively followed, and, in the absence of other methods of obtaining news, the happy idea was conceived and adopted of sending over from Paris dolls dressed in the prevailing mode, which enabled the ladies of St. James's to keep abreast of the times. When Lady Lansdowne was in Paris, in August, 1727, she sent to her friend Mrs. Howard, Lady of the Bedchamber to Queen Caroline, a doll dressed to show the Paris fashions exactly. "I have sent you," she writes, "a little young lady dressed in the Court dress, which I desire you would show to the Queen, and when she has done with it, let Mrs. Tempest have it. She was dressed by the person that dresses all the princesses here." The Mrs. Tempest referred to was a noted milliner, to whom the present would be very acceptable.

The frequent recurrence of the word "nightgown" in descriptions of dress, seems very odd to modern readers. Even in the eighteenth century

* R. Steele, *The Plain Dealer.*

it was never used to express what we mean by a night-gown. When Frederick, Prince of Wales, was married, in 1736, the bride's dress, which was of superb lace, is described as a night-gown. The term is often used for an evening gown. "I have got the laces, and the suit of night-clothes I have pitched on for you are charming," writes Mrs. Delany to a friend, in 1737, not meaning by "night-clothes" garments to sleep in, but to wear in the evening. The Countess of Shaftesbury, referring to Lady Ranelagh's marriage, wrote to Sir John Harris, M.P., that "Lady Ranelagh's clothes were extremely fine and pretty," and that "she had a straw-coloured night-gown with silver and colours that is extremely pretty, which cost thirty shillings a yard; and at Lady Romney's rout last Monday, she had on a white and gold." Dean Swift writes to his friend, Mrs. Howard, about sending her a piece of Irish plaid, at eight shillings and three-pence a yard, for what he calls a night-gown. "When the Princess asks you where you got that fine night-gown, you are to say it is an Irish plaid sent you by the Dean of St. Patrick's." Another correspondent of Mrs. Howard describes a lady as putting on "her broad-girdled calico gown and striped night-clothes to look decent upon the death of her mother." The night-gown was also used interchangeably with the sacque (spelt also "sack") for half dress. In the *Lady's Magazine* for March 1773, what is called undress as distinguished from full dress is given as follows: "Night-gowns or sacks with small aprons."

Patching was in vogue throughout the century. It enjoyed a very long run of favour. We went further than the French, who considered it only a vanity for the young and fair, while in England women of all ages and aspects patched. "I have often counted fifteen patches or more, upon the swarthy, wrinkled phiz of an old hag, three-score and ten upwards," writes that penetrating, but far from polite observer, Misson. Patching was turned to political use when party spirit ran high in the days of Queen Anne, and a lady showed her preferences by the patches on her face. "About the middle of last winter, I went to see an opera at the theatre in the Haymarket," writes Addison, "where I could not but take notice of two parties of very fine women that had placed themselves in the opposite side boxes, and seemed drawn up in a kind of battle array one against another. After a short survey of them, I found they were patched differently; the faces on one hand being spotted on the right side of the forehead, and those upon the other, on the left. I quickly perceived that they cast hostile glances upon one another; and that their patches were placed in those different situations, as party signals to distinguish friends from foes. In the middle boxes, between these opposite bodies, were several ladies who patched indifferently on both sides of their faces, and seemed to sit there with no other intention but to see the opera. Upon inquiry, I found that the body of Amazons on my right hand were Whigs, and those on my left, Tories; and that those who had placed themselves in the middle boxes were a neutral party, whose faces had not yet declared themselves. These last, however, as I afterwards found, diminished daily; insomuch that I observed, in several of them, the patches, which were before dispersed equally, are now all gone over to the Whig or Tory side of the face."

Altogether, it was a trying period, this eighteenth century, for the face. The complexion underwent as much treatment as the hair, and was put on with the gown, with infinite pains. Every conceivable kind of rouge and white, lip-salve and wash, was brought into requisition, and a lady's toilet-table with its "Dutch Pink," "Bavarian Red Liquor" to produce a blush, and Chinese paints, was as dangerous for a novice to meddle with as a chemist's laboratory.

> "The ladies of St. James's
>   They're painted to the eyes!
> Their white it stays for ever,
>   Their red it never dies.
>
> "The ladies of St. James's
>   They are so fine and fair,
> You'd think a box of essences
>   Was broken in the air." *

Wash-balls were in constant use, and a common ingredient in their composition was white lead, mixed with rice and flour. This was used for the best wash-balls. Nobody was troubled in those days by a knowledge of the injurious properties of white lead, and it was diligently rubbed into the skin as if it had been the most harmless of rice powders. Bismuth was also freely used. As the phenomena of disease were little understood, and the science of medicine was in an empirical stage, many people must have suffered a good deal from mysterious ailments which were attributed to anything but the right cause. Common wash-balls were less harmful than the more expensive ones, being made principally of whitening, flour, ground rice, and tallow soap. The coloured wash-balls were very risky articles. Vermilion, which was compounded in England, and was cheaper than carmine, was very much used, as was also red lead for adulterating the carmine. Yellow ochre, verdi-

* Austin Dobson, *Poems of the Eighteenth Century*.

gris, and amber were among the mixtures for the complexion. Another objectionable substance used for face-washes was quicksilver boiled in water, which was said to produce a "fine lustre to the cuticle," and to be perfectly innocuous when not mixed with salts. It was more specially recommended for various diseases of the skin.

There were also oils, and what were called perfumed foreign butters, of which the chief ingredient was lard scented with orange and jessamine. China supplied various pastes for the face. There was black eyebrow colour, a red mixture for the cheeks, a pearl powder for the neck, and a coloured wool of a delicate blush tint. India sent us a root from which lip-salve was made, mixed with suet and certain oils. A Danish cosmetic was much lauded. It was a wonderful mixture, compounded of many juices and waters, borax, vinegar, bread, eggs, and the heads and wings of pigeons. By its use the Danish ladies, it was asserted, retained the bloom of twenty-one at fifty.

There were many perfumed waters known, some of which came from Spain, Portugal, and Italy, and others which were made here, like lavender-water, and rose-water. A great many foreign soaps were in use—soaps from Spain and France, Italy, and Turkey—as well as the home-made Windsor and

Bristol soaps. But soap was shunned by some beauties, who relied on their creams and pastes. They avoided washing the face, arms, and hands altogether—except with their wash-balls,—for fear of impairing the whiteness of the skin, which, no doubt, was extremely sensitive to the action of soap and water after the constant treatment it underwent from chemical compounds.

One device for whitening the hands and arms was the wearing of dogskin and chicken-skin gloves.

> "Come, but don't forget the gloves,
> Which with all the smiling loves,
> Venus caught young Cupid picking
> From the tender breast of chicken;
> Little chicken worthier far
> Than the birds of Juno's car,
> Soft as Cytherea's dove,
> Let thy skin my skin improve;
> Thou by night shalt grace my arm
> And by day shall teach to charm." *

There were manicures even in those days. A certain male professor who announced that he could impart to the nails a most elegant shape attracted such an immense number of patrons among the fair sex that for about two years he was incessantly employed, and lived in princely style. One day he disappeared, leaving behind him debts to the amount of three thousand pounds.†

---

* Anstey, *The New Bath Guide.*
† Archenholz, *Picture of England.*

False eyebrows were put on complete, and occasionally with startling results. A lady who wore artificial eyebrows, which seem to have been laid on with some adhesive substance, was one warm day playing in the card-rooms at Tunbridge Wells. She happened to pass her handkerchief over her face, and in doing so inadvertently removed one of her eyebrows from its place, and left it sticking in the middle of her forehead. The gay company broke into a titter in which the unconscious lady joined, not in the least comprehending that she was herself the object of mirth. Not one of the other ladies present had the humanity to inform her of her misfortune or lead her from the room, but the laughter becoming more general, and whispers going round the circle, attracted the attention of the lady's husband, who presently discovered that all eyes were directed towards his wife. As soon as he perceived what had happened he rushed up to her, and revealed the dreadful calamity. The horrified lady was borne away in a fit, during which she lost three false teeth as well as her eyebrows.

Cosmetics could not avail against the ravages left by that scourge of our ancestors—small-pox. It was indeed a disease to be dreaded.

"Lo the small pox whose horrid glare
Levell'd its terrors at the fair;

> And rifling every youthful grace
> Left but the remnant of a face.
> Each former art she vainly tries
> To bring back lustre to her eyes.
> In vain she tries her pastes and creams
> To smooth her skin or hide its seams." *

The fashion of painting the face, which was common on the Continent as well as in England, was a Chinese custom. In 1766 an ordinance was published at Vienna forbidding women to paint. Women of the Western world rivalled those of the Eastern in the elaboration of the arts of the toilet. Hair-dyes were much used, for there was a constantly changing fashion in the colour of the hair. In 1775 golden hair lost all its admirers, and ladies who unfortunately possessed locks of the forsaken colour were directed how to change the hue by using elder-berries and red wine.

In the second half of the century dress took a somewhat different form. The large hoops were generally reserved for full dress, and for undress or half dress small hoops were worn. But the hoop declined very slowly, and complaints of its inconvenience were rife in 1780. Men grumbled that it was impossible to walk in the streets without being obliged to take to the road, because the hooped ladies occupied the whole pavement.

* Goldsmith, *The Double Transformation*.

Satirical people averred that the staircases of ordinary houses were too narrow to admit of a lady passing up and down, unless she went sideways; that tables were too small for a mere family party if there were three or four daughters; that the paternal purse was sorely stretched to provide sufficient quantities of stuff for the distended petticoats of the womankind of the household, and that the whole scheme of domestic life required changing. It was in this same year, 1780, that the large hoops were worn for undress as well as full dress, the fashion varying from season to season; and the following year brought in the large Rutland hoops.

In 1782 a change was observed in France. The Queen, Marie Antoinette, appeared at Versailles, one day in April, in a long white satin robe without a hoop, and this style immediately became the fashion. The Queen's gown was made with short wide sleeves, and she wore it as a morning robe. The next year hoops were almost completely abolished from polite society in England. But we had not seen the last of them. Back they came in 1784, as large as ever, and, as if to make up for the slight put upon them, were now decked with fresh ornaments and trimmings of feathers.

> "Let your hoop in its form much resemble a bell
> Your train hang behind somewhat more than an ell,"

was the advice to a lady of fashion in 1786.

All this time waists were varying their position. They were sometimes short and sometimes long.

> "The length of waist too vile appears
> It lifts the shoulders to the ears."

What are described as narrow shapes—in other words, tightly laced figures—were always aimed at, wherever the waist was placed. Tight lacing was very general, and young, growing girls were squeezed into artificial shapes, and their unformed figures filled out with "bolsters" and pads to make them look fashionable. A lady who was bemoaning the evil of tight lacing observed to a gentleman of her acquaintance that she should like to see all advocates of stays put into the stocks. "No, madam," he replied, "they should be set in the stays." Bodices were sometimes long, with the stomacher forming the front, as in the time of the Second Mary, only pointed in front instead of rounded. But whether the bodice was long or short, a thin, narrow figure was esteemed as the model of beauty, and the stout, broad people compressed themselves as well as they could into the decreed shape. The style of sleeve was much the same from the end of the seventeenth to the last decade of the eighteenth century. It was always an elbow sleeve for full dress, with ruffles of lace, or with the chemisette sleeve showing underneath—sleeves which Swift describes as "tuck'd halfway up the arm."

It is curious to find, in 1781, a gown worn called a "Poloneze," or the "Cumberland" gown, after the Duchess of Cumberland. It was not quite like our modern "polonaise," as it was not draped up in loops at the back, but had a train five yards long. A few months later comes in a gown drawn well to the back, showing the sides of the hoop petticoat, more after the fashion of the polonaise of later days, except for the train, which had been reduced by a couple of yards. The polonaise worn in France at this time—or perhaps it would be more correct to say, one of the varieties of that garment—was exactly like our polonaise with the back drapery caught up instead of falling in a train. In 1781 we find the prototype of another modern fashion in the long cloak with three little capes.

> "Let your gown be a sacque, blue, yellow or green,
> And frizzle your elbows with ruffles sixteen."

The sack was very much like the modern tea-gown, and quite as popular—more so in fact, for it was worn by all classes. "Pray let there be some alteration in the ladies' sacks, for I am quite tired of seeing every lady's woman and housekeeper drawling about with them just the same as their ladies have on, made exactly in the same taste, and sometimes in a higher; what I would propose is for servants to have no trimming. Let theirs drag upon the ground, to make amends for that deficiency, fourscore or a hundred yards or more, in proportion to the ingenuity and trouble they must be at to hold them up. Ladies of quality who don't always mind dress so much as a pert chambermaid, should wear theirs short, with one flounce at the extremity, reaching to another upon the petticoat, which may be made either of the same silk as the sack, gold and silver net, ermine, embroidery, sable, velvet of different colours, ornamented in full dress with jewels."* If "ladies of quality" had taken to wearing their sacks short the chambermaids would soon have copied them. There would have been no charm about a sack, however long, to a "lady's woman" unless it was worn by her mistress.

The opinions expressed by foreigners visiting England were very favourable as regarded the faces and figures of the English. One writer observed that there were not to be found in any country so

* *Lady's Magazine*, 1773.

many handsome persons of both sexes as in England. But the dress they thought very careless. M. Grosley, in his *Tour to London*, writes: "So sensible are the English ladies of their beauty that they neglect their dress, and are little solicitous about adorning their persons. A lady, when at home, generally wears a dishabille suited to the economy of her house. If she happens to make her appearance in a morning in St. James's Park, it is in a short gown, a long white apron, and a hat, and she is attended by a waiting-maid dressed as elegantly as herself. At public assemblies diamonds and lace adorn the sex, and then they make a distinguished figure. The care of dressing, that of dressing the hair above all, is observable only in a small number of ladies, who, thinking, no doubt, that they have occasion for it, have resolution enough to go through all the operations of the hairdresser. The country life led by these ladies during great part of the year, and the freedom which accompanies that way of life, make them continue an agreeable negligence in dress, which never gives disgust."

It seems as if M. Grosley, whose book was published in 1772, must have visited England some forty years previously, when Swift wrote, in his *Metamorphosis of the Town*—

> "This fashionable dishabill
> Has long prevail'd and longer will,
> For why, this candid country dress
> Does native innocence express."

Fashions in England were very much affected by the whims of certain great ladies who led the mode. "The Duchess of Rutland," says the *Lady's Magazine*, in December, 1783, "is expected to invent something new soon after Christmas; and the charming Lady Jersey is expected with a budget of Parisian fashions." "De Englishe! poor barbarians, dey know no more of de dress but to cover dere nakedness. Dey be cloded, but no dressed," said Mademoiselle d'Epingle.*

Every lady carried or wore a fan. It was an indispensable part of her costume. The eighteenth century witnessed the apotheosis of the fan. From the days of Queen Elizabeth downwards the fan had been steadily making its way, and to quote the flowery words of M. Octave Uzanne, which are as applicable to England as to France, the fan now "enters into the physiology of the feminine toilet, with the patch-box, the scent-bottles, the amber perfumed powders, and all the delicate arms of woman got ready by the Loves." The fan was used to express everything: political sentiment,

---

* Steele, *Grief à la Mode*.

party preference, approval of the latest opera, the last new book, were all denoted by pictures on the delicate gauze or silk of the jewel-mounted fan. The coquette turned the fan into a complete armoury of weapons with which to subdue admirers; and to know how to flutter the fan properly was as much a part of polite education as to make a graceful curtsy. An eighteenth-century poet writes of a—

> " Neat lady that is fresh and fair
> Who never knew what belong'd to good housekeeping care,
> But buys several fans to play with the wanton air,
> And seventeen or eighteen dressings of other women's hair."

It was customary at dances for ladies to throw their fans down on a table, and for the gentlemen to advance, each choose a fan, and invite the owner to be his partner. Fans varied with the times, like other articles of dress. They were very large in Queen Anne's reign. During the revolutionary period in France, when the large " heads " declined in England, fans, too, diminished in size. At the end of the century there was a strong leaning towards classic models, and gods and goddesses, the heroes and heroines of Greek mythology, were favourite subjects for fan-painting. All kinds of scenes and legends found their way on to the fan, until, as a correspondent wrote to one of the fashion journals, a lady hardly knew whether to blush before or behind her fan. And she had so many fans, suited to all occasions, that great care had to be exercised when dressing to see that she had put on the right one. How embarrassing it would be if the fantastically painted fan intended for the opera were taken to church; or the fan depicting revels, meant for a ball, accompanied the caller on a visit of condolence to a house of mourning!

The muff became more and more common, and grew larger and larger as the century advanced. French ladies at one time were fond of carrying tiny dogs in their muffs, and these muffs were called *chiens-manchons*. This fashion does not seem to have extended to England, but the muff was quite as general an article of dress as in France. When muffs were first worn in France, about the end of the sixteenth century, they were made of velvet and satin, trimmed with fur; but by the time the muff became naturalized in England, it was more commonly made entirely of feathers, or more often of fur.

> "Where's my dear delightful muff?
> Muff, my faithful Romeo's present!
> Tippet, too, from tail of pheasant!
> Muff from downy breast of swan!"

Bearskin and goat's-hair muffs were a good deal worn, and they were exceedingly large, which atoned in some measure for the want of proper covering for the arms. In many of the outdoor winter costumes there is no protection for the arms except the gloves, which reached to the elbows. A velvet tippet, with long ends edged with fur like the muff, made a pretty, but not very serviceable mantle. In the descriptions of fashions for full evening dress in 1795, a swan's-down muff is included, and in 1799 white muffs were considered full dress. A muff seems now an odd adjunct to an evening costume, though fur trimming has lately edged its way into ball and dinner gowns.

A great change came over costume during the last decade of the century. Both the head-dress and hoop were abandoned, and dress was modelled on quite different lines. Mrs. Delany was right when she foretold the downfall of the huge hoops and head-dresses. "I expect soon," she wrote in 1746, "to see the other extreme of thread paper heads and no hoops, and from appearing like so many blown bladders, we shall look like so many *bodkins stalking* about." This was exactly what took place, only not quite so early as Mrs. Delany expected.

The upheaval of 1789 ushered in a new era.

France took the classic type as her standard of fitness—falling very far short of her ideal,—and we in England followed suit. Elaboration gave place to simplicity, or, more correctly speaking, to studied simplicity, for imitation is never without effort. From being excessively wide, gowns became narrow and clinging. The waist was rather short, but had not yet risen to the armpits; the sleeves were quite tightly fitting, reaching to the elbow, and without any ruffles. There was nothing to give any appearance of fulness or width about the dress in any part. The figure was defined by the bodice, but not compressed. There were no "narrow shapes," or stiff stays and stomachers. It was as trying a style for the stout and broad, as the previous mode, but one admirably adapted to set off a graceful figure. Women had not for a long time enjoyed such perfect ease. Some dresses were made quite on the Grecian model, with the chiton buttoned on the shoulders, but not confined by any girdle at the waist. The style of hair-dressing being also *à la Grecque*, completed the illusion of a classic figure. Trains were worn for Court costume, but the ordinary full-dress gown was not extravagantly long. Coloured shoes seem to have been universal among fashionable folk, both indoors and out. The period of strong, wet-resisting foot-gear had not arrived. Ladies were only supposed to walk when the weather was fine and the streets were dry. For evening wear, satin shoes were used, and for day wear, morocco, in all sorts of bright colours. For instance, among the day costumes for the early spring of 1795, red morocco slippers are included, to be worn with a chintz gown, a short black satin cloak, and a black velvet bonnet. The pelerine crossed at the waist in front, and with the ends knotted at the back, appears among the fashions for 1798; and there must have been a short mantle worn about this period as an out-door garb, for the French adopted a kind of cape which they called *un mouchoir Anglais*. It only just covered the shoulders, and came down in a point to the waist at the back, like a folded handkerchief.

Among the changes which the Revolution introduced into costume, was a sudden liking for what was termed "fire colour." This terrible hue, so full of dire suggestion, appeared in everything. There were fire-coloured silk shoes, fire-coloured ribbons in the caps, and fans with fire-coloured sticks.

It was about this time that a silly fashion prevailed in England of wearing riding-habits for morning out-door dress. It began, of course, among *bonâ fide* riders, who, for convenience' sake, put on their habits some time before they were going to ride, and perhaps took a walk, or paid a visit in their equestrian garb. The custom spread among those who never mounted a horse in their lives, and ladies took to going to church in riding-habits and round hats. The appearance of these hats in church was severely reprobated by a writer in the *Lady's Magazine*, who considered them " very irreverent in a place of divine worship; for although long custom has established that the ladies' heads shall be covered with bonnets or hats in church as well as elsewhere, yet I do not conceive that this privilege extends to the wearing of riding-hats, which are part of the riding-habit, and which do not differ in appearance from the round hats worn by men, but never worn by men in church. I am of the opinion holden by the *Spectator* in one of his papers, that we ought to keep fashions as much as possible out of the church; there are so many other places, indeed, such as the opera, the theatres, balls, concerts, ridottos, routs, dunes and hurricanes, where we may be as fashionable, and as properly fashionable as we please, that I would be for reserving a plain simplicity and a decency in garb for our places of religious worship." The most fashionable riding-habits were made of dark blue cloth opening over a white vest, or, as they called it then, a waistcoat.

Feathers were worn in the hats, which were trimmed with gold lace and fringe. Some ladies wore scarlet habits. Lace ruffles were added as to ordinary dresses.

The French, in their absurd passion for copying the antique, paid no heed to the climate and conditions of their country, but walked about in light garb, suited only to the warm airs of the South. They went far beyond their model in their eagerness, and quite transgressed the bounds of decency, appearing in the promenades and public gardens in gowns which barely draped, and certainly did not clothe the body. These were the extremists, but the majority contented themselves with exposing their feet. This is the picture Carlyle gives of the Frenchwoman of 1794: "Behold her, that beautiful adventurous Citoyenne! in costume of the Ancient Greeks, such Greek as Painter David could teach; her sweeping tresses snooded by glittering antique fillet; bright-dyed tunic of the Greek women; her little feet naked, as in Antique Statues, with mere sandals, and winding-strings of riband—defying the frost."

The costumes worn by English ladies out-of-doors, at this time, though never so outrageous as those seen in France, were extremely unsuited to our treacherous climate. The gowns were open at the neck, back and front, and ladies might be seen walking about at Ranelagh and other fashionable resorts without even a scarf. Their arms, to which exposure was of less consequence, were completely encased in long gloves, which came up to the sleeves. There was an entire absence of trimming about the gowns; they were absolutely plain—their whole beauty consisted in the cut. When these unadorned gowns were of white muslin, which was very fashionable, they had a charming air of rusticity a little spoilt, perhaps, by the small train, without which, however, they would have looked awkward. While the white muslin mania lasted, young and old alike donned muslin gowns and broad sashes. The matron of fifty boldly assumed the dress of the maid of fifteen; but this was less remarkable in an age when little girls wore their petticoats as long as their mothers, and boys were dressed exactly like men.

To modern notions there is a singular confusion in the eighteenth century between out-door and in-door costume, between full dress and half dress. Low-necked gowns and thin fancy-leather shoes—red, blue, and pink—were, as has been seen, worn out-of-doors. Sometimes, it is true, there were large comfortable cloaks trimmed with fur for winter; but often there was nothing over the dress but the tippet, which barely covered the shoulders; and it must be remembered that none of the modern comforts in underclothing existed.

A fashionable walking-costume for December, 1799, according to one of the fashion journals, consisted of a white muslin dress, a pink silk cloak covered with black crape and trimmed with black lace, a fancy hat with ribbons, and a brown bearskin muff—the only article in harmony with the season. Winters in London at the end of last century must have been very different from those we experience, to induce any one to don such a costume for walking. The same white muslin is used for full dress, only it is trimmed with lace and satin.

Silk pelisses, spencers, and black velvet cloaks were among the out-door winter garments; but, instead of the cloak, which was long and wide, and really seemed as if it might keep out the cold, there was sometimes substituted what was called a fancy Barcelona handkerchief, wadded or furred, but a very poor protection compared with the cloak. A white sarcenet robe is put down as a suitable morning dress for February, 1800; and in December of that year the white muslin robe again appears as a walking-dress. What spirited defiance of the nipping cold is implied by this wearing of white muslin in December! Truly our ancestors were heroic to the point of madness in their devotion to fashion.

> "What art, O Fashion, power supreme below!
> You make us virtue, nature, sense forego."

Judging from contemporary caricatures and the satirical remarks that appeared in the daily journals, there was a section of fashionable society whose aim it was to go as scantily clothed as possible—like the French. One lady is said to have appeared at a ball in Dublin, in the year 1796, in flesh-coloured pantaloons with only a gown made of gauze over. Underclothing of all kinds was reduced to a minimum, all considerations of health and comfort being ignored by the *haut ton*. What excited more ridicule than anything was the absence of waist; for some of the gowns were as shapeless as a child's loose pinafore. These were called "petticoat dresses" and "waggoners' frocks," and were perfectly straight from top to bottom, with not even a girdle to define the figure. Caricatures and songs described ladies as having lost their waists, and indeed their bodies, and being unable any longer to eat or drink. However, at the close of the century, waists reappeared, and with a tendency to become long.

Another fashion, and a very innocent one, which was much laughed at, was that of carrying a reticule instead of having a pocket in the gown. The hanging bag, made to match or to harmonize with the dress, has been revived more than once without exciting any comment, but it appeared supremely absurd to writers on costume in the eighteenth century. It was odd that such a trifle should have attracted so much notice, and it seems as if Fashion were, after all, not so outrageous as she is represented.

There was a strange mingling of styles and tastes, a struggle between the ancient and the modern, the simple and elaborate, the natural and the artificial. Greek fillets and towering feathers, muslins and diamond necklaces, the chiton and the high-heeled shoe, were jumbled together in the wardrobe of the society belle. She was not an "architect in dress," and she was guilty sometimes, in her "Gothic ignorance," of "mixing the orders." Are we not doing the same now, with our revivals of contrasting periods and our modifications and adaptations to suit modern taste?

CHAPTER V.

GENTLEMEN'S DRESS.

Elaboration of a gentleman's toilet—Coats and cravats—The beau—Beau Nash and Beau Brummel—The fashions ridiculed—The macaronies—The muff—Wearing of swords—Seaside fashions—Changes—Introduction of plainer style.

> "Now quite a Frenchman in his garb and air,
> His neck yok'd down with bag and solitaire,
> The liberties of Britain he supports,
> And storms at place-men, ministers, and courts;
> Now in cropt greasy hair and leather breeches
> He loudly bellows out his patriot speeches."
> JENYNS S., *The Modern Fine Gentleman.*

"CURIOUS reader, picture to yourself a town-bred bachelor, with flowing wig, brocaded waistcoat, rolled-silk stocking, and clouded cane, marching forth to take a survey of Bartholomew Fair in the year 1701." Let us hope that the rain kept off, and that the streets were tolerably free from mud, or his beautifully curled wig would soon become lank and his fine silk stockings splashed. A "town-bred bachelor" was very careful about his

toilet. Though not the first, it was the most engrossing occupation of the day. Before he left his bed, he sipped his chocolate, read his letters, thought over his engagements, very likely had an interview with a tailor or a hatter, and received a visit from some acquaintance who was obliged to rise betimes. Then he betook himself to the important business of dressing. To this he gave serious and undivided attention; and not until he was satisfied that the powder was well settled on his wig, that his ruffles were in order, the ends of the lace cravat exactly adjusted, and that his snuff-box was filled, did he issue forth from his chamber. His deportment was dignified, as befitted the nature of such a costume. A hurried manner would have been altogether out of keeping with his attire. If he were pressed for time he must not appear to be so; somebody must be kept waiting. Young and old alike acquired a certain stiffness of bearing, and their attire showed an odd mixture of gravity and foppery. The long coats and wigs imparted an air of soberness; the ruffles and buckles, the lace and embroidery, gave a touch of levity.

In name the several parts of male costume were much the same as now, but in cut and colour they greatly differed. Coats were very long-skirted, and the sleeves were what would be thought baggy now, with wide cuffs. "The young fellows have drop'd down the flaps of their coats very near as low as the clocks of their stockings, so that scarce anything of the leg is seen but ancle; and they seem pulling them still lower and lower, that they may be more and more like petticoats, which the women are gratefully tucking up shorter and shorter."* Waistcoats were very long too. The modern waistcoat is a poor shrunken thing compared with the waistcoat of the last century, which, *minus* the sleeves, was almost equal to a present-day coat.

There were no such things as flannel or coloured cambric shirts among gentlemen. A shirt was made of the finest white lawn, with lace ruffles down the front and at the wrists. The cravat, in the earlier part of the century, was of lace also—good point lace; and so expensive were these cravats, that even young men of fashion seldom had more than two at a time. Gentlemen showed a great fondness for lace, and nearly buried their hands in deep lace ruffles. They also had gloves edged with lace, which were often carried instead of being worn. The knee-breeches were almost hidden by the coat, but the delicately coloured silk stockings were in full evidence.

* Steele, *The Guardian*.

> "With stockings of silk, nothing less can such please,
>   Bind his legs round with silver just an inch above knees,
>   Hang a tassel to that or else it won't do,
>   And in length it must reach half way to the shoe."

The chilly but dainty fashion of wearing silk stockings and shoes had lasted on from the previous century. Boots were not generally worn, except for riding. "Lord Peterborough is here," writes Lady Hervey to Mrs. Howard, "and has been so some time, though by his dress one would believe he had not designed to make any stay; for he wears boots all day, and, as I hear, must do so, having brought no shoes with him."

The wig really did away with the need for any other head-covering, but a gentleman always carried his hat, as a matter of form, when he did not wish to put it on. More often he was to be seen with his—

> "Pretty black beaver tuck'd under his arm,
>   If plac'd on his head might keep it too warm."

A good hat was rather an expensive article, and was considered important enough to be left among the bequests in a will. It was not easy to make the hat rest securely upon the wig, and the "cock" of the hat was a very important matter. There was the military cock; the Denmark cock, which came in when the King of Denmark visited

England in 1768; the mercantile cock; Nivernois hat with small flaps attached to a flat crown; and the theatre hat, which could be folded up.

> "But what with my Nivernois hat can compare
> Bag-wig and laced ruffles and black solitaire?"

There was a curious custom of hiring hats by subscription. Three hats valued at a guinea each could be hired for £1 14s. 6d. per annum; and four hats, value £1 4s. each, would be let out at the rate of £2 6s. per annum. Cocked hats were ridiculed as the "Egham," "Staines," and "Windsor," after the triangular posts which pointed to those places.

The fashion was constantly changing. In 1770 hats were round, and in the latter part of 1772 fashion magazines describe the hat as "rising behind and falling before;" a few months later large hats were giving way to medium-sized ones, and in the last quarter of the century round hats came into fashion again, especially for morning wear. Cocked hats were always worn by boys. The three-cornered cocked hat had its downfall with the Revolution of 1789, which materially affected the style of dress in England.

The skirts of the coats were at first stiffened with wire to make them stand out well, but this fashion was given up in the second half of the century. "The skirt of your fashionable coat forms as large a circumference as our petticoats," writes Steele in a letter to the *Spectator*, under the guise of a female correspondent; "as these are set out with whalebone, so are those with wire, to increase and sustain the bunch of fold that hangs down on each side."* Lace cravats, which were so popular under the name of Steinkirks, were abandoned for a simple black ribbon tied in a bow.

> "And what can a man of true fashion denote
> Like an ell of good ribbon ty'd under the throat?"

A Steinkirk was a lace cravat, fastened so loosely as to seem folded rather than tied, with the ends passed through a buttonhole of the coat. Ladies wore them, too, arranged with more appearance of care, and the soft folds of lace made a very pretty finish to the neck. These cravats were called Steinkirks after the battle of Steinkirk, when some of the French princes, not having time to perform their elaborate toilet before going into action, hurriedly twisted their lace cravats about their necks. The fashionable world eagerly followed their example. It is rather curious that the Steinkirk should have been popularized in England, where the name must have been a bitter remembrance.

* Steele, *Letters to the Spectator*, 1711.

Then followed the cambric stock, fastened behind, and after that the muslin cravat, which was very large and required great nicety in folding to make it set properly. When the muslin cravat came in, the shirt collar rose, the ruffles down the front vanished; we were entering upon an era of plainness.

> "What straitness in the skirts appears!
> The neck is rais'd up to the ears,
> Which to the flattest shoulders give
> A rising fulness."

Our fashions were not exact copies of the French; they were partly home-grown. Grosley, in his *Tour to London*, speaks of the English fashions as being diametrically opposed to those of France; but, at the same time, considers that there was an attempt at imitation of the French. Fashion news came to England from Paris by all sorts of round-about ways. Sometimes a wealthy English lord brought a new mode back with him from a visit. Individual members of the aristocracy exercised much more influence on dress in the eighteenth century than is possible now, and a well-known figure in society could do more to affect costume than all the tailors put together. A gentleman of the *beau monde* discussed the modes seriously with his tailor:—

"Your gallant and his taylor some half a year together
To fit a new sute to a new hat and feather,
Of gold or of silver, silk, cloth, stuff or leather,
And is not Old England grown new?"

The beaux had a club where they met to compare costumes and invent new fashions.

Grosley describes the relations between the fashionable worlds of London and Paris in the following terms: "A mode begins to be out of date at Paris, just when it has been introduced at London by some English nobleman. The Court and the first-rate nobility immediately take it up; it is next introduced about St. James's, by those that ape the manners of the Court; and by the time it has reached the city, a contrary mode already prevails at Paris, where the English, bringing with them the opposite mode, appear like the people of another world. The little hats, for example, at present so fashionable in France, begin to be wore by the nobility, who borrowed the model from Paris; by degrees the English will come at the diminutive size; but the great hats will then be resumed at Paris. This holds good in general, with regard both to men and women's apparel."

The typical figure of the eighteenth century is the beau, or macaroni. He reflects the fashions for us like a glass. For "his first care is his dress, and next his body, and in the fitting these together consist his soul and all its faculties." What better exponent of costume could there be than one to whom it was a life study? Steele writes of "the difficulty in arriving at what ought to be esteemed a 'fine gentleman.' That character has been long wholly engrossed by well-drest beaux, and men of sense have given up all pretence to it. The highest any of them contend for is, the character of a 'pretty gentleman;' for here the dress may be more careless and some wit is thought necessary; whereas a fine gentleman is not obliged to converse further than the offering his snuff-box round the room." In another letter he says: "The town swarms with fine gentlemen. A nimble pair of heels, a smooth complexion, a full bottom wig, a laced shirt, an embroidered suit; a pair of fringed gloves, a hat and feather; any one or more of these and the like accomplishments ennobles a man and raises him above the vulgar in a female imagination. On the contrary, a modest, serious behaviour, a plain dress, a thick pair of shoes, a leathern belt, a waistcoat not lined with silk, and such like imperfections degrade a man, and are so many blots in his escutcheon. The gilt chariot, the diamond ring, the gold snuff-box and brocade sword-knot are no essential parts of a fine gentleman, but may be used by him, provided he casts his eye upon them but once a day." *

The business of beaux, says Misson, is to hunt after new fashions. "They are creatures compounded of a periwig and a coat laden with powder as white as a miller's, a face besmeared with snuff, and a few affected airs." But there were famous beaux in the eighteenth century who ruled manners as well as dress, and whose refinement of taste sensibly improved their circle. Beau Nash, of Bath celebrity, did a great deal to reform the manners and appearance of the company who frequented the Assembly Room of that fashionable watering-place. He compelled the country squires who had been in the habit of coming to the balls in their top-boots which they wore for riding, to appear properly attired, like other gentlemen, in low shoes and silk stockings. But it was not until he had employed all the weapons of ridicule that the change was effected. "To push his victories, he got up a puppet show, in which Punch came in booted and spurred, in the character of a country squire. He was introduced as courting his mistress," who desires him to pull off his boots. "'My boots,' replies Punch, 'why, madam, you may as well bid me pull off my legs! I never go without boots.

* Steele, *The Guardian.*

I never ride, I never dance without them; and this piece of politeness is quite the thing at Bath. We always dance at our town in boots, and the ladies often move minuets in riding-hoods.' Thus he goes on, till his mistress, grown impatient, kicks him off the stage. From that time few ventured to appear at the assemblies in Bath in a riding-dress; and whenever any gentleman, through ignorance or haste, appeared in the rooms in boots Nash would make up to him, and bowing in an arch manner would tell him that he had forgot his horse."* One wonders that the gay company at Bath did not frown the country boors out of countenance without any assistance from the great master of the ceremonies. The belles of St James's could not have enjoyed the company of men in heavy boots, the spurs of which caught in their dresses.

Beau Nash's own costume is hardly to be taken as a specimen of the times, for he followed his own special taste, and his attire was a combination of fashions. Nobody then wore white hats, but Nash always wore one, to secure it from being stolen, as he said. He called himself a beau of three generations, for he was born in the reign of Charles II and died in that of George III.

* O. Goldsmith, *Life of Richard Nash*.

> "Long reign'd the great Nash, this omnipotent lord,
> Respected by youth and by parents ador'd;
> * * * * *
> But alas! he is gone, and the city can tell
> How in years and in glory lamented he fell:
> * * * * *
> If true what philosophers all will assûre us
> Who dissent from the doctrine of great Epicurus,
> That the spirit's immortal: as poets allow,
> If life's occupations are follow'd below;
> In reward of his labours, his virtue and pains,
> He is footing it now in the Elysian plains,
> Indulg'd, as a token of Proserpine's favour,
> To preside at her balls in a cream-colour'd beaver." *

Another famous despot, the social lion of his age, was Beau Brummel, the favourite companion for many years of the Prince of Wales, afterwards George IV., who, next to Brummel, was the best-dressed gentleman of the day. The secret of Brummel's incomparable costume lay in the elaborate care which he lavished on every detail. The toilet of a gentleman was always a long process in those days, but Brummel regularly spent three hours every morning in the hands of his servants. He had three hair-dressers, who attended respectively to the front, back, and sides of his head. His great achievement was the cravat tie; it was designed for him by a clever portrait-painter, and Brummel, contrary to general custom, had his slightly starched.

* Anstey, *The New Bath Guide.*

If the first tying were not perfect, the cravat was rejected and a fresh one taken. He wore three cravats, or neckcloths as they were called, every day, the last one being put on after he came from the opera or theatre, before he went to supper or cards. Cravats were then made of muslin. He had three shirts daily. What a horror he would have had of false fronts and cuffs, and all such economies to which ordinary people resorted! "Sir, I say you put upon me when I first came to town about being orderly and the doctrine of wearing shams to make linen last clean a fortnight, keeping my clothes fresh and wearing a frock within doors."* Beau Brummel might have indited the following *Reflections on a Clean Shirt*. He, if any one, owed a tribute to the skill of the laundress.

> "Hail, bright invention! by whose friendly aid,
> This shirt once more so decently is made!
> Goddess of arts and industries, arise,
> Assert thy legal empire in the skies.
> With smiles behold the salutary rub,
> And crown the labours of the daily tub,
> But bless that friend to Covent Garden bloods
> Who first invented proper soap and suds."

It can easily be believed that Beau Brummel's washing-bills were pretty heavy. Even when, in the years of his decadence, he was living at Caen

* Steele, *The Conscious Lovers.*

with an income of eighty pounds a year, he spent more than thirty of it on his laundress. One cannot blame Brummel for his exquisite appreciation of cleanliness, which amounted to a passion. It was too uncommon a virtue in days when oils, essences, powders, and scents were far more used than soap and water.

There was a constant fire of ridicule directed against the fashions of the day in the periodical literature, but especially against the feminine toilet. A lady, referring to some satirical remarks upon her own sex, says, with much justice, that they would be equally applicable to the men. " I defy the most strict examiner to find any one folly in us that they do not abound with in an equal degree. If we have our milleners, mantua makers, and tire-women to take up our time, have they not their taylors, barbers, aye, and their face-menders too, to engross as much of theirs? Are there not as many implements on the toylet of a beau as there can be on one of the greatest coquet among us? Does he not take the same pains to attract, and is as much fond and proud of admiration? Are not the men in general affected with every new mode, and do they not pursue it with equal eagerness? Are there any of the fashionable diversions (call them as absurd as you will) that they do not lead us into by their example? If we affect a little of the rusticity of a country maid in our walk and motions, do not they shoulder into all public places with the air and mein of a German hussar? If we sometimes put on the *romp*, I am sure they act the part of the *ruffian* to the life."

The *Spectator* proposed that a repository of fashions should be established. It was to be a building with apartments for both sexes, so "that every one who is considerable enough to be a mode, and has any imperfection of nature or chance which it is possible to hide by the advantage of clothes, may, by coming to this repository, be furnished herself and furnish all who are under the same misfortune with the most agreeable manner of concealing it: and that, on the other hand, every one who has any beauty in face or shape may also be furnished with the most agreeable manner of showing it." Its secondary purpose was to keep young gentlemen at home who go abroad "to make or improve a fancy for dress."*

The beaux wore their waistcoats very open to display a good deal of their fine shirts, and there was a silly custom of throwing back the coat in all weathers for the same purpose. This was ridiculed in the *Spectator*, in a humorous letter, in which the

* Steele, *Letter to the Spectator.*

writer averred that the dreadful coughing of the gentlemen who thus exposed themselves quite disturbed, not only the parson in the pulpit, but the actors at Drury-lane Theatre, and drowned the music of the opera at the Haymarket. If the gallants are so anxious to show their shirts, much better wear them outside their coats, when at least " people will be persuaded that there is no cheat in their shirts, but that they are all of a piece,"—which was not the case, the front being of the finest linen and the back of a coarser kind. Or if that will not do, " let them wear some certain badge, or, if you please, let them have a ticket hanging down their breasts, like a crucifix, with this motto, ' I have a fine shirt upon me ;' and if any wear this whom they suspect, let them open his breast and satisfy themselves. And till this be done, let none of them go either to the church, opera, or play-house, whereby you will oblige all the ladies that frequent those places."

Shoe-buckles were a very expensive item in a gentleman's dress.

> " His buckles like diamonds must glitter and shine,
> Should they cost fifty pounds they'd not be too fine."

The large buckles composed of jewels often cost quite a fortune. A rich nobleman once offered to give Peg Woffington a pair of shoe-buckles which cost four hundred pounds, if he might place them himself on her shoes. Sir John Spencer, who lived in the middle of the century, and was one of the richest men of the time, had a pair costing the prodigious sum of thirty thousand pounds. Buckles, says William Hutton, came in with William III. and liberty, but they were small then, about the size of a horse-bean. They took all sorts of shapes, and became bigger and bigger, until they half covered the front of the shoe. Every one wore shoe-buckles —men, women, and children,—and on small feet the great square buckle, which was a fashionable shape, looked heavy and out of proportion.

After a time the fashionable world tired of its expensive buckles: they were inconveniently large, and shoe-strings took their place. This caused great commotion among the buckle-makers, who petitioned the Prince of Wales, in 1791, to do something to revive their declining trade. When the Revolutionists in France set about altering costume, they did away with shoe-buckles and fastened their shoes with strings. The Minister Roland, one day in 1793, was about to present himself to Louis XVI. in shoes with strings. The punctilious master of the ceremonies, scandalized at having to introduce a person in such a state of dishabille, looked despairingly at Dumouriez, who was present. Dumouriez replied to the gesture with the words, "Hélas! oui, monsieur, tout est perdu."

The original macaronies, as the beaux were called in the second half of the century, were members of Almack's Club, where the dish macaroni was first introduced. Mr. Lewis Wingfield ascribes this honour to the "Sçavoir Vivre" Club. The younger and more dashing members of the club, who were distinguished for the richness of their dress, went by the name of "Macaronies," and the term was soon applied to the fastest set of town gallants and beaux. "The worst gallant in nature is your macaroni; with the airs of a coquette, the manners of a clown; fear keeps him in some awe before the men, but not one spark of passion has he at heart to remind him of the ladies." There were two classes of macaronies—the "bloods" and the "frolics," whose names aptly represented their character and behaviour in the public streets.

The macaronies soon introduced changes into the style of dress—cutting their waistcoats quite short, so as to reach to the waist only, while their coats were shorn in like manner, made square in front, and with tails at the back—in fact, the shape of the modern evening coat. Short waistcoats and short-fronted coats seemed very foppish to an age accustomed to long, flapping waistcoats and coats with skirts. White waistcoats, sometimes made of silver tissue, were worn for evening dress. Blue was a favourite colour for coats at all times of the day. Beau Brummel always wore a blue coat in the evening, with black pantaloons, which he had made to button right down to the ankle. For full dress the macaroni attired himself in a coloured velvet coat of some delicate shade, lined with satin, or perhaps faced with ermine. At other times his coat was of variously coloured cloth, claret, blue, brown, or whatever the fashion might decree for the season. Black was never worn, except for mourning. Complete suits of light-coloured silk were worn by the smarter men for balls.

Dress coats, which differed more in material than in shape from morning coats, were apparently not *de rigueur* at all public balls; for Miss Catherine Hutton, giving an account of a particularly fashionable city assembly held at Birmingham, in 1783, writes: "The men were chiefly in dress coats, with their hair in bags; those who were not, wore cloth coats, trimmed with narrow gold lace."* In winter, short cloaks or fur-lined coats were worn out-of-doors. Party spirit displayed itself in the colours of men's

* *Reminiscences of a Gentlewoman of the Last Century.*

costume. Yellow waistcoats and breeches denoted a staunch Whig; a scarlet waistcoat, ornamented with gold buttons, and a pair of black silk breeches, a supporter of Pitt.* The buttons of the coats were very fanciful and sometimes curiously engraved.

In cold weather the man of fashion was never without his muff, hung round his neck by a ribbon, and trimmed with a bunch of ribbons in the centre.

> "For I ride in a chair, with my hands in a muff,
> And have bought a silk coat and embroider'd the cuff;
> But the weather was cold, and the coat it was thin,
> So the taylor advis'd me to line it with skin."

A very quaint and ingenious story is related concerning the origin of the muff. Mars, jealous of the love of Venus and Adonis, took the form of a wild boar, and in this guise fell upon and slew the beautiful youth. Venus, in despair, followed Adonis to the nether world to intercede with Persephone for his release from the realm of ghosts. Persephone compassionately arranged that Adonis should ascend to earth at stated times to revisit his beloved goddess. The change of temperature from the lower to the upper world was great, and Adonis found his fingers much chilled on first coming up to earth. Accordingly, it was ordained that the murderer, Mars, should be compelled to descend

* W. C. Sydney, *England in the Eighteenth Century.*

from Olympus and kill a number of sables, to make a warm covering for the hands of Adonis, who, like a true gallant, soon found other uses for his muff besides that of a mere hand-covering, and became expert in the art of toying with his new possession, making it as expressive of sentiment as the eyes.*

In France, in the time of Louis XIV., Court gentlemen used to carry muffs trimmed with bunches of ribbons, and sometimes the muff was a mass of ribbon and lace. It was always changing its shape, size, and quality; at one time big minever muffs were seen everywhere, and at another, tiny satin muffs lined with down. In England muffs were worn by both men and women during the Stuart Era, but they did not become a common feature of dress until the eighteenth century. It was about the year 1762 that, some obstacle arising to the importation of furs, feather muffs became popular in France, and were introduced into England. Muffs just then were very small. Walpole, writing to George Montague, says, "I send you a decent smallish muff that you may put in your pocket, and it cost but fourteen shillings." But in 1765 gentlemen, apparently, carried very large muffs; for a lady remonstrates with a gentleman with whom she was walking in the park for wearing such a

* *The Lady's Magazine*, 1780.

"monstrous" muff, of which he was particularly proud. Muffs were so commonly used by men that Dr. Josiah Tucker, Dean of Gloucester, wore his muff in the cathedral.

A story is told of a London citizen who was wont to go to church wearing, suspended from his neck, a white muff which he had bought in Paris. It happened that a maiden lady occupied the same pew, and was accustomed to bring her pet puppy to church with her. One morning, while the worthy citizen was occupied with his prayers, the little dog crept into his muff; and when the gentleman, all-unconscious of what had happened, tried to put his hands back into his muff, the little dog set up a violent barking. With some difficulty the intruder was shaken out, amid the merriment of the congregation and the indignation of the maiden lady, who thought her favourite was being treated with much disrespect. The muff, like the fan, was made to serve political purposes; and when party spirit was very pronounced in the time of Charles James Fox, the partisans of that statesman carried large muffs made of the fur of the red fox.

Gentlemen carried very long swords—sometimes diamond hilted—thrust beneath the skirts of the coat, as part of their everyday attire. A man of fashion wore—

> "A gold-hilted sword, with jewels inlaid,
> So the scabbard's but cane, no matter for blade."

Warren Hastings appeared at his trial with a diamond-hilted sword, which was taken from him before he knelt at the bar. Beau Nash abolished swords from the Bath Assembly Room because they tore the ladies' dresses and caused alarm. Quarrels were easily aroused in those days on trifling points of etiquette, and it required little incitement for swords to come flashing out of their scabbards. But there was no Beau Nash to rule fashionable London, and in the public promenades the swords were as troublesome as the ladies' hoops.

"I will tell you how I was served the other day in the Mall," writes a lady. "There were five of us perfectly well dressed; for my part, I had a new suit of cloaths on I had never wore before, and everybody says is the sweetest fancied thing in the world. To speak truth, we took up the whole breadth of the walk; unfortunately for me, I happened to be on the outside, when a creature, who I afterwards heard was a Dettingen hero, came hurrying along with a sword as long as himself, hanging dangling at his knee, and pushing roughly by me, his ugly weapon hitched in the pinked trimming of my petticoat, and tore it in the most rueful manner imaginable. I am so happy as not to be enough concerned for any of that sex to give myself any sort of pain, how ridiculous soever they make themselves. I only laughed at the Khevenhuller cock of the hat, so much the fashion a little time ago, and the fierce arm-a-Kembo air in a fellow that would run away at the sight of a pot-gun. As the poet says, 'All these things moved not me.' But as my whole sex, and myself in particular, have been aggrieved by swords of this enormous size, and the manner in which they are worn, I could not help communicating my thoughts to you on the occasion, which I beg you will not fail to insert in your next publication. If you are really as impartial as you would be thought, you will add something of your own to make the men ashamed of appearing in a country which, thank Heaven, is at present at peace within itself, as if they were in a field of battle, just going upon an engagement."* Swords continued to be carried up to 1786, after which they were worn only with Court costume.

In the latter part of the century it became fashionable to take an annual trip to the seaside, as it was to journey periodically to Epsom, Tunbridge Wells, and Bath. Life at a popular watering-place was, in one particular, precisely the same as it

* *The Female Spectator.*

is to-day; people went, not for health so much as for custom's sake, and spent their time in dressing and promenading. It was quite as necessary to be in the mode at Margate—which was one of the first places to draw visitors—as at Bath. Fashions were probably more extravagant and accentuated at the seaside than in London, for in August, 1787, the *London Chronicle* published a satirical paragraph of advice to a man of fashion relative to the correct costume for seaside wear: "For the morning provide yourself with a very large round hat. This will preserve your face from the sun and wind, both of which are very prejudicial to the complexion. Let your hair be well filled with pomatum, powder, and bear's grease, and tuck it under your hat. Have an enormous chitterlin to your shirt, the broader the better, and pull it up to look as like the pouter pigeon as you possibly can. A white waistcoat without skirts, and a coat with a collar up to your ears will do for an early hour; and if they say your head looks like that of John the Baptist in a charger, tell them you are not ashamed to look like an Apostle, whatever they are. Your first appearance must be in red Morocco slippers, with yellow heels; your second in shoes with the Vandyke tie; your third in Cordovan boots with very long rowelled spurs, which are very useful to walk in, for if you tear a lady's apron, it gives you a good opportunity of showing how gracefully you can ask pardon. Your fourth dress must be the three-cornered hat, the Paris pump, and the Artois buckle."

The style of coat introduced by the macaronies gradually became the prevailing fashion. After 1786, or thereabouts, the wide skirts of the coats were transformed into long tails. Coats were double-breasted, and so short in front as not to reach the bottom of the waistcoat by some three inches.

Buttons were very much esteemed as ornaments. They were very large, and of curious shapes and patterns. When buttons first came into use is uncertain; but in the last century they were exceedingly prominent on the dress of both sexes, but especially on that of men. The green cloth riding-coats, which French gentlemen took to wearing for morning costume in 1786, were furnished with large mother-of-pearl buttons. Cloth buttons were not made, but all sorts of metals and stones were in use. On the coloured velvet, silk, and cloth coats these big bright buttons were very striking. A certain debating club at Christ Church, Oxford, prescribed as the costume of its members a brown coat with velvet collar and cuffs and buttons, bearing the initials of Demosthenes, Cicero, Pitt, and Fox.* The members of a Cambridge club wore bright green coats, lined and bound with buff-coloured silk, and adorned with buttons on which the phrase *Sans Souci* was engraved.†

The taste for bright colours lasted right on to the end of the century. Although black coats *à la Révolution* were worn in 1790-91, they were deprived of their sombreness by being worn over scarlet and other brilliant-hued waistcoats and pantaloons. There was a great deal of gay dress during the Revolutionary period. Carlyle describes Robespierre as wearing on one occasion a sky-blue coat, a white silk waistcoat embroidered with silver, black silk breeches, white stockings, and gold shoe-buckles. Caricatures represent English Whigs dressed up in very gay attire in imitation of the Republican ministers whose principles they were supposed to favour. The fashion-books for both England and France show us gentlemen arrayed in light bright-green coats, and in coats faced with contrasting colours, in canary-coloured pantaloons and pink and buff waistcoats. Grass green had been a fashionable colour for gentlemen's coats in the fall of 1786. But still, a plainer style of dress was

* W. C. Sydney, *England in the Eighteenth Century*.
† *Ibid.*

creeping in, and little by little the stately foppery of the century was disappearing. The change worked from the head downwards. The man who wore his own hair, short, plain, and unpowdered, did not care about elaborate dressing. He liked the same ease and simplicity in his garments that he had acquired for his head-gear. With the giving up of wigs and powder came the fall of the cocked hat. A round hat took its place, a hat with a somewhat high crown and broad brim, but the legitimate ancestor of the nineteenth-century top-hat.

In England complaints were heard that there was no distinction between the dress of a peer and a peruke-maker, that it was impossible to tell a bishop from a baker, a duke from his footman. The commonalty, however much they tried to imitate the aristocracy, preferred seeing noblemen dressed in satin and diamonds rather than in the plain suits of their own class, and the lament of a *soi-disant* tradesman expressed a widespread feeling, animated by self-interest, and alarm about the possible decline of trade: "The last general mourning was a dreadful time to me. I made blunders every day. . . . If great men will dress like tradesmen and tradesmen like great men, it will be necessary to make a new law of fashion, by which it shall be decreed that slovenliness is the characteristic of nobility, and that lace and embroidery denote a tradesman. When that is fully established we may know how to proceed. . . . The greater part of the peers do not look like lords a dozen times a year, birthdays included, and common tradesmen look like lords all the year round."

CHAPTER VI.

Court dress—Its formality—No improvements suggested by sovereigns—Costliness and splendour of some Court costumes—"Birthday" dresses—Jewellery—Lace and aprons—Conservative character of Court dress—Fashionable amusements.

> "But pleasures are like poppies spread,
> You seize the flower, its bloom is shed."
> BURNS.

COURT dress, in the first half of the eighteenth century, was not markedly different from the fashionable dress usually worn on festal occasions. It was only a little more elaborate and sumptuous. When large hoops were in fashion, the hoops seen at Court on birthdays and festivities were enormous. If feathers were being worn as a head-dress, the feathers which adorned the head of a lady going to Court would be higher and stiffer than on any other occasion. Were pearls in favour as ornaments, a Court dress would be trimmed with ropes of pearls. When wigs, swords, and ruffles, light silk suits, and buckled shoes formed the ordinary full dress of a gentleman, his Court costume only differed by being more embroidered, belaced, and bejewelled. Court dress was, in consequence, pompous and stiff. All costume partook of that character in the earlier part of the last century, and there was no presiding genius at Court to order things differently. The artistic sensibility that marked the Stuart sovereigns was lacking in their successors, who patronized art, but had no æsthetic tastes. The uncompromising rigidity of the Dutch style was apparent in dress under William and Mary, and Queen Anne had no desire to alter or reform anything. She was a strong conventionalist, and liked to see the people about her arrayed in strict conformity with what was prescribed by custom. Certainly, some writers, as we have seen, credit Anne with introducing a low coiffure at a time when the head-dress was extravagantly high;* but if she really were responsible for that short-lived innovation, such action was contrary to her usual course.

The first two Hanoverians added a degree of dulness to society and ugliness to dress with their awkward manners and German tastes. As far as their influence went for anything it was depressing. Neither George I. nor George II. won any personal attachment: they were not in sympathy with the

* Cf. Chap. III.

people whom they were called on to govern; they were conscientious office-holders, and that was all. England never had sovereigns whose qualities and characteristics made so little impression. George III. and his Queen were much more in touch with their subjects; but they led a simple domestic life, and followed rather than initiated fashion. They were ridiculed and satirized for their homely habits and tastes. The royal pair were depicted by caricaturists doing their inexpensive shopping together in true Darby-and-Joan style. This brought forth the following lines from John Wolcot:—

> "And why, in God's name, should not queens and kings
> Purchase a comb or corkscrew, lace for cloaks,
> Edging for caps, or tape for apron strings,
> Or pins, or bobbins as cheap as other folks?
> Reader, to make thine eyes with wonder stare,
> Farthings are not beneath the Royal care."

It was not the Court that really guided the fashions. The English nobility arranged matters for themselves, taking France as their model. There were reigning belles in the eighteenth century who could have rivalled the beauties of the time of Charles II.—such as Lady Mary Wortley Montagu, the Duchess of Devonshire, the Duchess of Rutland, and Lady Jersey. They influenced fashion largely; but though they graced the Court, they belonged to society much more than to the Court. Lady Mary ought, perhaps, to be omitted from the list of fashion leaders, notable as she was in smart society. Curious stories were afloat about her habiliments. Pope, in his *Characters of Women*, writes of the ill agreement of "Sappho's diamonds with her dirty smock," and of "Sappho at her toilette's greasy task," —Sappho being a transparent disguise for the form of the learned Lady Mary. There is also a quaint tale told by Horace Walpole, which ends with a reflection on Lady Mary's toilet. A holy man once visited a poor woman, who entertained him to the best of her ability. In the morning, when the saint was about to take his departure, he gave the woman his blessing, and told her that whatever she should begin to do as soon as he was gone, she would continue to do all day long. Instead of trying to heap up riches, the woman went quietly about her everyday tasks. It happened that she had a piece of coarse cloth with which to make shifts for herself and child. She no sooner began to measure but the yard fell a-measuring, and there was no stopping it. The sun was setting before the woman had time to take breath. She was almost stifled, being up to her ears in ten thousand yards of cloth. She could have afforded, adds Walpole, to have sold Lady Mary Wortley's clean shift, of the usual coarseness she wears, for a groat halfpenny.

Lace was one of the most expensive parts of Court and fashionable dress. It was worn in large quantities under William and Mary, when the commodes and Steinkirks came in, and continued to be in great demand for "heads." For a King who had so little personal vanity, William spent large sums on lace for cravats and handkerchiefs, night-shirts and razor-cloths. The Queen was equally lavish in her outlay on lace. She spent nearly two thousand pounds in one year on handkerchiefs, combing-cloths, night-dresses, and other articles. So Queen Mary's lace was a very considerable item in the royal household accounts. Besides her head-dresses and aprons she wore quantities of lace on her dress. Portraits show thick ruffles of guipure round the neck of the gown.

Mary had a much more graceful appearance than her sister Anne. In her purple velvet bodice and train and minever stomacher encrusted with diamonds, and with the regal mantle falling from her shoulders, she was queenly and dignified. Whether in royal purple or in stiff brocade, she always had a great deal of her favourite guipure about her. The sleeves were made narrow at the top and wide at the elbow—almost exactly like the elbow-sleeves of twenty or five and twenty years ago—and were finished off with deep lace ruffles; not fastened to the sleeves, but forming part of a kind of chemisette. Queen Anne, also, spent large sums on lace, though the Flanders lace bought for her coronation did not amount to sixty-five pounds. But the Queen grew more extravagant afterwards, and ten years later she was spending upwards of fourteen hundred pounds for lace in one year. A lace handkerchief then cost something like ten pounds, and a Flanders laced head and ruffles about eighty pounds.

In Anne's reign distinctions began to be made between the lace produced in different cities, and instead of lace being generically termed "Flanders," we hear of "Brussels" and "Mechlin lace."[*] All through the century lace was an essential part of the wardrobe of fashionable ladies and gentlemen. It was too expensive for general use. George II. was very particular about his lace, and looked after his attendants to see that they provided him with fresh ruffles. It seems to have been the custom to sew the lace on to the shirt-sleeves, which necessitated frequent renewal, as the coat, being dragged over the ruffles, soon spoilt them. In France, for Court presentations, nothing

[*] Palliser, *History of Lace.*

but point lace was allowed.* There was point de France and point d'Alençon; but the French ladies preferred Brussels point for their head-dress lappets. The point d'Alençon was used for shirts and cravats. It had the advantage of standing washing well—a great consideration in days of snuff-taking. Valenciennes lace, which did not acquire a reputation until the eighteenth century, was also an accommodating lace, submitting gracefully to the trying process of "getting up," and was accordingly much in request. Being soft and delicate, it was peculiarly well fitted for wearing as neck-ruffles.

A great deal of lace was also used by the rich classes in France for bed-curtains, coverlets, and pillow-cases. The use of lace increased greatly in the eighteenth century, just as it did in England. Flounces of point lace were worn on Court dresses up to the end of the century, and triple lace ruffles. In England lace was much worn on underclothing by the royal family, and their linen was more expensively trimmed than the linen made for royal ladies at the present day. The princesses of the family of George II., when very young, were allowed eighteen day-shifts and eighteen night-shifts every two years, trimmed with lace at ten shillings a yard. As babies, they seem to have

* Lefebure, *History of Embroidery and Lace.*

been clothed in lace on grand occasions, and had for birthdays little lace suits worth from fifty to sixty pounds each.

The cost and splendour of some of the dresses worn at Court on *fête* days quite surpassed anything seen now. Even children wore diamonds. Princess Anne, for one of the birthdays, had an azure velvet coat made for her son, the little Duke of Gloucester, with button-holes encrusted with diamonds and buttons made of brilliants, to the grave disapproval of King William, whose dislike to his sister-in-law and all her doings was very marked. George II. wore a blue velvet coat with diamond buttons on one of Queen Caroline's birthdays, and a hat buttoned up with very big diamonds. At the marriage of the Prince of Wales, the King and several of the nobles wore suits of gold brocade, costing five hundred pounds each.

The ladies of the Court also wore a good deal of gold and silver brocade, and costly materials of a similar kind. In 1739, at one of the Court festivities, the Princess of Wales wore white satin covered with gold net; the Duchess of Bedford, a petticoat of green paduasoy thickly embroidered with gold and silver, while on the body of the gown was a mosaic pattern of gold facings. Lady Carteret wore velvet trimmed with silver flounces; Lady

Percival, white satin embroidered with gold and silver; Lady Dysart, a white satin embroidered petticoat, and a scarlet damask gown embroidered with gold and colours. Very startling patterns were devised for the embroidery of these Court dresses, which would astonish the Court milliners of the present day.

Mrs. Delany wrote, in 1740, describing a reception at the residence of the Prince of Wales: "The Duchess of Queensberry's clothes pleased me best. They were white satin embroidered, the bottom of the petticoat *brown hills* covered with all sorts of weeds, and every breadth had *an old stump of a tree* that run up almost to the top of the petticoat, broken and ragged, or worked with brown chenille, round which twined nasturtiums, ivy, honeysuckles, periwinkles, convolvuluses, and all sorts of twining flowers, which spread and covered the petticoat. Vines with the leaves variegated, as you have seen them by the sun, all rather smaller than nature, which makes them look very light: the robings and facings were little green banks with all sorts of weeds, and the sleeves and the rest of the gown loose twining branches of the same sort as those on the petticoats: many of the leaves were finished with gold, and part of the stumps of the trees looked like the gilding of the sun."

Jewels were plentiful enough at Court festivities. The Duchess of Portland, at a birthday, in 1742, wore a stomacher all diamonds, and a bouquet of coloured jewels. But English ladies could not rival the splendour of the Nabob's lady who came to the English Court wearing prodigious earrings of diamonds and pearls which quite sheltered the sides of her face, twenty rows of pearls round her neck with pendants reaching to her waist, a diamond girdle an inch broad, ten rows of pearls round the wrists, and ten rows round the arms.

It was not at all uncommon for ladies to borrow jewels of each other for the Drawing-rooms. The French ladies did the same. Their Court attire was always very splendid, and the etiquette of the French Court was very precise in matters of dress. A lady who was to be presented went " in the most magnificent stuffs, tricked out with the finest point laces of her wardrobe, and glittering with all the diamonds she could collect from the jewel-boxes of her relations." It was the custom in England for mothers to lend their jewels to their daughters even when both mother and daughter were present at the same festivity. Miss Carteret appeared at Court on the Prince of Wales's birthday, in 1738, in all her mother's jewels, although Lady Carteret was there herself. Mrs. Delany, who attended the same birthday, borrowed a buckle of Lady Sunderland for her stays. There was no attempt on the part of the borrowers to pass off the jewels as their own. It would have been useless, for the jewels belonging to a great lady were as well known to society as their owner. Even queens did not disdain to borrow. Lord Hervey, writing of the coronation of George II., says, "The dress of the Queen on this occasion was as fine as the *accumulated* riches of the city and suburbs could make it; for besides her own jewels (which were a great number and very valuable) she had on her head and on her shoulders all the pearls she could borrow of the ladies of quality at one end of the town, and on her petticoat all the diamonds she could hire of the Jews and jewellers at the other."

At a Court festivity, one day in 1766, there was present a lady wearing jewels worth fifty thousand pounds. For a diamond necklace two or three thousand guineas would often be paid. The royal Order of the George was made in diamonds. Lord Cowper, in 1787, recklessly ordered a thousand pounds' worth of diamonds to be sent to him by post—a method of conveyance he was accustomed to employ. They were lost in transit, and, being uninsured, Lord Cowper was compelled to pay the jeweller, whose responsibility was considered to cease when the stones were despatched. That diamonds should be sent through the post in such reckless fashion argues an almost insolent trifling with precious stones, begotten of undue familiarity. Royal weddings were, of course, the occasion *par excellence* for the display of diamonds. Queen Charlotte, wife of George III., wore a necklace and stomacher of diamonds on her wedding-day worth three thousand pounds, and a tiara of diamonds at her coronation. The bridesmaids all wore diamond crowns.

Marriages were also, naturally, times for bringing out jewels and rich stuffs. George the Second's daughter, who wedded the Prince of Orange, had for her wedding-gown a white damask, embroidered in embossed gold. "On one side of her head she had a green diamond of a vast size, the shape of a pear, and two pearls prodigiously large, that were fastened to wires and hung loose upon her hair; on the other side small diamonds prettily disposed; her ear-rings, necklace, and bars to her stays, all extravagantly fine, presents of the Prince of Orange to her. The Prince of Orange was in a gold stuff, embroidered with silver; it looked 'rich, but not showy. The King was in a gold stuff, which made much more show, with diamond buttons to his coat; his star and George shone most gloriously. The

Queen's clothes were a green ground, flowered with gold and several shades, but grave and very handsome; her head was loaded with pearls and diamonds." One of the Princess's attendants was in a pink satin suit trimmed with silver, that cost fifty guineas.

Some of the gowns seen at Court were certainly more striking than beautiful. Picture a lady in a black velvet petticoat "embroidered with chenille, the pattern a *large stone vase* filled with *ramping flowers* that spread almost over a breadth of the petticoat from the bottom to the top; between each vase of flowers was a pattern of gold shells and foliage, embossed, and most heavily rich; the gown was white satin, embroidered also with chenille mixt with gold ornaments, no vases on the *sleeve*, but *two or three on the tail*."

The ermine petticoats worn under velvet gowns must have been very hot wear at a crowded Drawing-room, but the materials more generally used were damask, satin, tissue, and paduasoy. Sometimes shaded silks were used. There is frequent mention of lustring, or lutestring, a fine silk made in all colours, both plain and flowered. Embossed trimmings were very much used, and the gowns were frequently quite stiff with gold and silver tissue. The formal style of dress, the tightly fitting bodices with long waists, and the high stays, which produced a perfectly artificial shape, were all in harmony with the unpliable brocades which were so much in request. Very stately and magnificent the Hanoverian princesses must have looked in their gold and silver tissue gowns, their enormous damask hoops, and their purple velvet mantles edged with ermine. The Princess Royal, daughter of George II., is described as wearing, on one birthday, a white paduasoy embroidered with gold; Lady Hartford was in a "blue manteau embroidered with gold," one of the princesses in a pretty combination of pink damask trimmed with silver, and the Prince of Wales in a "mouse-coloured velvet, turned up with scarlet and very richly embroidered with silver." These flowered and silvered materials were all French fashions. Mrs. Delany describes a French gown of her own, for which she gave seventeen pounds, made of dark green silk, brocaded with pale-coloured flowers.

Wedding-gowns were very similar to the gowns worn at Court on birthdays. The Miss Carteret already mentioned, who was married in 1733, wore a white satin gown, embroidered with silver. The guests were in white and coloured satins, also embroidered in silver, and the bride had all sorts of damasks and flowered silks in her trousseau. Later on, when muslin was as much worn as satin by the fashionable world, we find a bride arrayed in a silver muslin night-gown, and sprigged muslin apron trimmed with lace. An heiress who was married in 1788 was attired in what is called a white satin "levee" and coat, with a white satin hat, bridal veils not having taken the place of hats and bonnets. The bridesmaids were daintily dressed in white muslin, with snowdrops and myrtle for adornments. This wedding, although a fashionable one, took place at eight in the morning; but weddings were celebrated at all sorts of hours in the eighteenth century. One of Walpole's friends, married in 1759, whose wedding is described in his *Correspondence*, was married "just before dinner," and the fashionable dinner hour was three or four o'clock. Nollekens relates that his wife wore on her wedding-day "a sacque petticoat of the most expensive brocaded white silk, resembling network, enriched with small flowers, which displayed in the variation of the folds a most delicate shade of pink, the uncommon beauty of which was greatly admired. The deep and pointed stomacher was exquisitely guimped and pinked, and at the lower part was a large pin, consisting of several diamonds, confining an elegant point lace apron." *

* *Nollekens and His Times.*

Aprons went out of fashion in the first half of the century, but some ladies insisted on keeping them. Until Beau Nash took the lead at Bath, aprons were worn at the assembly balls, but that social despot had a great dislike to aprons, whether of muslin or of the finest Mechlin lace. They were only fit, he said, to be worn by Abigails, and he forbade any lady to come to balls in an apron. In spite of this mandate the Duchess of Queensberry had the temerity to appear one evening in a lace apron. Nash marched straight up to her Grace, snatched off the apron, and threw it over to the ladies'-maids, who were sitting at the back. The good-humoured Duchess took no offence but smilingly submitted to the indignity. On another occasion she was not so complaisant. An order was issued that aprons were not to be worn at Court. The Duchess, disregarding the injunction presented herself at one of the Drawing-rooms in a beautiful lace apron. The lord-in-waiting refused to admit her, whereupon the Duchess, with more spirit than courtesy, tore off the offending article and, throwing it in the face of the astonished lord, went on her way.

Some of the fashionable ball gowns of the last decade of the eighteenth century would look extremely odd now. A short time ago an attempt was made to bring in long sleeves for evening bodices, which looked very incongruous with the low necks, and did not win any popularity. In 1791 we read of long sleeves being made to ball gowns, which was very strange at a period when short or at least elbow sleeves were so much worn in the day time. These long-sleeved gowns were not cut very low on the shoulders, and were finished off with a frill of lace round the neck. Different materials were often used for the skirt and bodice, and the sleeves were of one colour and the bodice of another. "A white satin body with pink satin sleeves, and a spotted book-muslin skirt over pink satin," made a pretty ball dress. Very particular people had hand-painted muslins, but this was an unusual extravagance.

Crape was a favourite material for Court dresses, especially in the last quarter of the century. It was also used a good deal for caps. In 1786 the Princess Royal, on the King's birthday, wore a green and silver tissue gown covered with crape, and trimmed with oak leaves and real acorns. Another dress worn on this occasion was pale yellow, covered with crape and silver, and trimmed with puce flowers. The Lady Spencer, of the Marlborough family, wore a petticoat of white crape and silver, and a pale blue gown trimmed with silver fringe. Gentlemen had their gala suits for birthdays, and the Prince of Wales on this particular birthday wore an orange silk serge, embroidered in silver, and covered with spangles. The coat sleeves were made of silver tissue; so was the waistcoat, and the whole costume was studded with blue and white stones and buttons to match. Black feathers were occasionally worn in the head-dresses. In 1791 spangled and embroidered crape was the material most generally used for the Court dresses of ladies. Again, in 1793 and 1794, the fashion-magazines state that many white crape petticoats were worn on the royal birthdays. In the latter year the prevailing colour for the other parts of the costume was yellow, while green was favoured by the gentlemen. The following year, one-third of the gentlemen who appeared on birthdays were in regimentals, and pale light colours were affected by the ladies. At the first Drawing-room held in that year by the Princess of Wales the gentlemen wore either striped embroidered silk suits or light-mixture cloths. Being the month of May, lilac and rose-colour appropriately prevailed among the ladies.

Velvet turbans, black and coloured, with very high plumes, were worn at Court. In 1798 "high feathers" were prescribed by the authorities for Court dress. The Court seemed determined to retain the worst abuses which disfigured costume. Big hoops, very large in front, were worn, the ugliest variety of the hoop ever seen. The princesses wore enormous hoops—which, at this time, were not worn anywhere except at Court and in remote parts of the kingdom where the fashions had been late in arriving. Over the ungainly hoop the gown was looped up, no train being worn, so that, with the high feathers and short, distended, bunched-up skirts, a Court lady was the reverse of elegant.

Except that hair-powder ceased to be used by the Queen and the ladies who attended Drawing-rooms, there was hardly any improvement in the style of Court dress up to the end of the century. The Court, like the country, was slow to reform, and clung to the traditional modes. The simpler style which prevailed in other circles was not thought befitting the formality of Court life. The Prince of Wales, whose taste in dress was his only unimpeachable characteristic, did not effect any changes as long as the reins remained in the hands of the old King.

As for social life it was much the same all through the century. Breakfasts, auctions, dinners, routs, dances, and cards filled up the day of the fashionable world. Madame Boccage, who visited

England in 1765, writes with great appreciation of the pleasant breakfast parties of literary circles. "Well-served breakfasts bring together an agreeable mixture of natives and foreigners. We breakfasted to-day at Lady Montagu's, in a closet lined with painted tapestry well furnished with Chinese furniture. A long table covered with a cloth, white as snow—quantity of brilliant vases containing coffee, chocolate, biscuits, cream, butter, toasted bread, in many different manners, and exquisite tea—the best is drank in London." The mistress of the house and the English ladies round her in their white aprons and little straw hats—a curious costume—greatly excited the visitor's admiration.

But dancing and card-playing were the two main amusements of the Court and the fashionable world. Cheating at cards was not only tolerated, but admired as clever and smart. The absorbing love of whist which prevailed in the higher ranks of society is well brought out in one of Horace Walpole's keen criticisms: "The Kingdom of the Dull is come upon earth—not with the forerunners and prognostics of other-to-come kingdoms. No, no, the sun and the moon go on just as they used to do, without giving us any hints: we see no knights come prancing upon pale horses, or red horses; no stars, called wormwood, fall into the Thames, and turn a third part into wormwood; no locusts like horses, with the hair as the hair of women—in short no thousand things, each of which destroys a third part of mankind: the only token of this new kingdom is a woman riding on a beast, which is the mother of abominations, and the name on the forehead is whist; and the four and twenty elders, and the woman, and the whole town do nothing but play with this beast. Scandal itself is dead, or confined to a pack of cards; for the only malicious whisper I have heard this fortnight is of an intrigue with the Queen of Hearts, and the Knave of Clubs."

As for dancing, it was, like cards, a diversion for grave and gay alike. Men did not stand out half the programme in those days: they were as keen for the dance as their fair partners. A certain caricature depicted a State cotillon with the Lord Chancellor dancing on Magna Charta, and another statesman on the National Debt. The excessive love of company among the idle classes was thus bemoaned by the *Female Spectator:* "Ladies run galloping in troops every evening to masquerades, balls, and assemblies, in Winter, and in the Summer to Vauxhall, Ranelagh, Cuper's Gardens, Mary-le-Bow, Sadler's Wells, both old and new, Goodman's Fields, and twenty other such like places, which in this age of luxury serve as decoys to draw the thoughtless and unwary together." Among the "twenty other such like places" the opera certainly deserves mention. Very stringent were the regulations about the dress of those occupying boxes. Stalls were not invented then, the pit taking all the floor up to the stage. In the hall was stationed a master of the ceremonies, who scrutinized the audience as they passed in, and if any gentleman who was not in full dress with silk stockings, shoes, and folding hat attempted to enter a box, he was stopped and refused admittance.

There was a very marked difference between the habits and manners of the various grades of society in London. The West End and the City, the man of fashion and the man of business, were very far removed from each other. "Each part of the town is a separate republic, and has, in point of society, its laws, its customs, and even its languages; for not only the same words have different meanings in the different parts of the town, but many phrases which are current in everybody's mouth at St. James's, are quite unintelligible on this side of St. Paul's Church; so that a man who distinguishes himself by his wit and vivacity in a city assembly or coffee house is quite as much at a loss in an assembly in St. James's Square, or a coffee house in St. James's Street, as if he was just arrived from a foreign country. . . . If anything can equal the contempt which a man of fashion has for a citizen, it is that which the citizen has for the man of fashion; only with this difference, that the man of fashion is uniform and consistent in his contempt, and that the citizen is so far otherwise that he attempts to imitate those very customs and manners which he affects to contemn."

CHAPTER VII.

Military dress—Wigs and cocked hats—Lace cravats—Uniforms more settled—Colours and shapes—Cost of military clothing—Unpopularity of the Army—Abuses in Army and Navy.

> "Intestine war no more our passions wage,
> And giddy fashions bear away their rage."
> POPE.

BY the eighteenth century military dress was settling down into a more regular form, though still subject to the variations of fashion. It followed civil costume in directions where imitation was least desirable. If the soldiers of the Stuart armies cherished their flowing curls, the soldiers of Queen Anne and the Georges were no less careful of their powdered tails and clubs. Nothing could have been more inconvenient and absurd than the elaborate hair-dressing to which officers and privates alike had to submit. The waste of flour was enormous, and the waste of time in preparing those elaborate heads still more grievous. To encumber men in active service with such a toilet seemed madness. Then the high, cocked hat, which required coaxing to make it keep in its place, was a very unsuitable head-gear for military purposes, but it was adopted because it happened to be the fashion of the day, and lasted until the Duke of Wellington introduced a hat with a lower crown, which he found better suited for wearing on horseback. After the battle of Ramillies, hats were worn with what was called the Ramillies cock. Cocked hats could be worn in all sorts of ways, and the particular angle chosen by the soldiers on that famous day was immediately taken as the correct pattern, not only by military men, but by civilians as well. The cocked hat, laced, was at that time generally worn throughout the army, and the other forms of head-gear introduced were peculiarly unfortunate, both as regarded appearance and comfort. "A good strong hat, well laced," is the description given of the hat to be provided for a foot soldier. A laced hat for a sergeant cost ten shillings; a private's hat, which had less lace, was rather cheaper. Some officers took to wearing broad-brimmed hats with feathers, but those were exceptions. In the eighteenth century, soldiers were allowed to wear beards.

> "The soldier's beard doth march in shear'd
>   In figure like a spade,
> With which he'll make his enemies quake
>   And think their graves are made."

Armour had now ceased to be worn, owing to the different style of warfare and the universal use of firearms. Consequently the colours adopted for the different regiments, and the form of dress, became more noticeable. The Guards wore scarlet faced with blue, and the regiments of the Line, red with different facings. The coats were of the square type peculiar to that period. Big heavy boots wide at the top were worn by the cavalry, and shoes with long black gaiters by the infantry. Officers wore point lace cravats like the beaux of St. James's, and as much silver lace about their coats as they could put on. The chief difference between an officer and a private was that the latter substituted white tape for silver lace.

The artillery raised by George II. had a blue uniform, faced with red. The King himself, when reviewing the Guards, one day in 1727, wore a uniform of grey cloth faced with purple, though to what regiment that costume belonged is not very clear. But the colours varied about this time. Some companies of dragoons seem to have worn green waistcoats and breeches, afterwards changed to white. The Fifteenth and Sixteenth Light Dragoons, which George III. called the King's and Queen's, wore scarlet and blue like the Guards, and, instead of the aiguillette worn on the left shoulder by the dragoons of George II., they were adorned with epaulettes on both shoulders. Their scarlet cloaks were lined with white, and had blue capes. Heavy jack boots reaching to the knee marked the dragoon.

In one particular, effect was more studied than economy, in the clothing of the Army. White leather and white woollen breeches must have been very extravagant wear. Indeed the foot-guards were at one time paid a penny a day extra, in consideration of the frequent washing required by these white breeches and gaiters. The trumpeters had scarlet coats trimmed with yellow lace, and hats with scarlet feathers, until, in 1784, the coats were changed to blue. In 1786 the general officers of the Army are described as wearing at Court their new uniform of scarlet cloth, lined with white, with blue cuffs and scollops of gold lace. The sash, in the time of George III., was worn round the waist; in the preceding reign it had been worn over the shoulder. The Cavalry tied it at the right, and the infantry at the left side. Hessian boots came in during the reign of George III., and were worn with light leather pantaloons.

The Grenadiers had been for some time wearing pointed Prussian caps, but in the early part of the reign of George III. these were exchanged for the hot, heavy bearskin. The Fusiliers were also given the bearskin cap, and in time of peace were allowed new caps every two years.

The shape of the coat was changed several times during the century. At first the coats were all square and wide-skirted. Then the skirts, like those of the civilians' coats, shrank into tails, these tails being very long. Up to 1778 the soldiers' coats were flapping about their ankles, and their waistcoats came down to the middle of the thigh. Everything seemed devised to make the soldier as uncomfortable as possible. He was encumbered either with heavy jack-boots reaching nearly up to his knees, or with gaiters fastened with a long row of buttons. His coat-tails were dreadfully in his way in muddy weather. His neck was girt up in a stiff leather collar, and on his elaborately curled and powdered hair he balanced, with difficulty, a laced cocked hat. None of the great generals of the eighteenth century even tried to reform military dress, or to render the soldier's toilet easier and quicker. They took no account of the daily annoyances to which the men silently submitted. Only the clamorous received attention.

In the reign of George I. the Guards revolted at the quality of the linen supplied them, and threw their shirts over into the royal garden, calling them Hanover shirts. The Duke of Marlborough, into whose garden some of the shirts were thrown, apologized to the mutinous regiment for the indignity put upon them, and the obnoxious shirts were publicly burnt at Whitehall.

One curious piece of economy was studied in providing the soldier's clothing. His first year's coat was made to serve as a waistcoat, the second year. The waistcoat of a private in the infantry seemed never to have been new except when he first entered the service, but always to have been made out of a half-worn coat. "One year indeed I have a new coat, next year I make a wescoat on't, the third year a pair of britches, and after that it makes a cap." The attire of a sergeant in an infantry regiment cost a little over £5; of a drummer, about £3 12s.; a corporal and a private, a little under £2. Of course the clothing of a recruit, who had double of everything new, came to a good deal more. About half a crown was allowed to a sergeant for having his old coat transformed into a waistcoat, and one shilling to a private.

A very full inquiry into the state of the clothing of the Army was made, by a committee specially appointed, in 1746, abuses having been rife among the regiments serving abroad. It was then brought out, from the evidence of army tailors, that the cloth used for the coats of marching regiments was from four shillings to five and sixpence a yard. Kersey breeches cost about one and fourpence a yard; stockings were thirteenpence a pair, and shoes from three shillings to three and ninepence. "The Commissary of the Stores makes my Captain pay four and sixpence for an Irish pair of shoes worth two and sixpence." The making of a waistcoat for a private was fourteenpence if laced, and a shilling if plain. One tailor stated that he should charge more for turning an old coat into a waistcoat, than for making a new waistcoat. For making the coat the charge varied from two shillings for a private's coat up to eleven shillings for a drummer's. Red and yellow cloth seem to have been much the same price. It was strongly suspected that the colonels of regiments made hundreds of pounds out of fresh clothings, it being customary for the contract to be made between the colonel and the clothier. If this were the case, the tailors never betrayed the colonels.

The Army was an extremely unpopular Service certainly, in the early part of the century, pay being very irregular. All sorts of devices were resorted to for getting recruits, and bounties had to be offered to fill up the gaps in the regiments. The Duke of Schomberg, when he wanted to raise a regiment of dragoons, promised forty shillings as levy money to men who had already served, and to raw recruits thirty shillings, with complete accoutrements in both cases. Justices were empowered in Queen Anne's reign to levy able-bodied men who had no other employment, and a volunteer was offered a bounty of forty shillings. Places were bought and sold with shameless audacity, and captains, colonels, and majors created with surprising rapidity, under the very eyes of the Government.

In the Navy things were worse. Men who knew nothing of naval matters, and had never been to sea in their lives, acquired the nominal command of ships and received the pay, the real work being done by some experienced subordinate. These were the kind of captains described as "young spruce Beauish non-fighting officers, often to be seen at Man's Coffee-house, loaded with more gold lace than ever was worn by a thriving hostess upon her re petticoat, all ladies' sons, of a fine Barbary ᵗ ᵗ, dance admirably, sing charmingly, speak French fluently, and are the darlings of their mothers; have large pay for little service, are kept at home by the interest of their friends to oblige the ladies, and hate the thought of going on board ship because their nice noses are unable to endure the smell of tar or the stink of belg water; besides, they are as much afraid of dawbing their cloaths, as they are of venturing their carcases."

CHAPTER VIII.

COSTUMES OF THE COMMONALTY.

London fashions in the country—General dress of the middle classes—Umbrellas: their introduction—Costume of the fashionable world copied by the commonalty—Costume of certain callings.

"Opinions like fashions descend from those of quality down to the vulgar, where they are dropped and vanish."—SWIFT.

"You will be surprised to hear the conveniency of hoop-petticoats is got to the red ones in the country, and that Kate and Joan are longer getting over a stile now, than a fine lady is getting out of her coach. The parson is forced to begin an hour later for them. Susan had the misfortune last week to hang so long on the top of one of the stiles, that Ralph discovered the upper half of her green stockings was yellow, and has since left her."* This was written in 1725. The gentle sarcasm of the word "conveniency" is very apt. A hoop-petticoat

* *Letters to the Tatler and Spectator.*

in the dairy among the great pans of milk and tubs of butter, or in the farmyard terrifying the fowls and ducks, must have been a ludicrous spectacle. Twenty years later Mrs. Delany avers that dairymaids were wearing large hoops. By that time the so-called "conveniency" had become fully established in rural England.

Fashion news travelled down into the provinces slowly and with difficulty, by stage coach, over miry roads, by the uncertain medium of the post-boy with the news-letters, on the pillion with a London lady paying a rare visit to her rustic cousins, or in the lumbering chariot of some family rich enough to pay a yearly visit to the Metropolis. People who could afford the "month's polishing" in town that poor "Mrs. Hardcastle"* so much desired, served as fashion models for their less fortunate neighbours, who were reduced to all sorts of shifts to devise "heads" and gowns *à la mode*. The Vicar of Wakefield's daughters hailed "modish" ladies from London as heaven-sent visitants. The inmates of quiet country houses who never went to routs and assemblies, auctions and public gardens, and whose only promenade was a retired lane, or the skirt of an unfrequented common, were eager to keep up with the times. But unless they were deft with their

* *She Stoops to Conquer.*

needle, and possessed the knack of turning and altering, they must have been at a great loss how to copy the London fashions, when, at length, they arrived, rather stale. The milliners and dressmakers in country towns could hardly have been very skilled in the last century. They had so little experience and practice. In the households of the landed gentry there were sewing-women who did all that the London modistes failed to supply, and women of the middle classes managed for themselves. Needlework was still a necessary accomplishment in the last century, though people were even then waking up to the fact that it did not satisfy all the aspirations of women.

The hoop-petticoat was, no doubt, thought very fine in the country. It had the merit which many fashions did not possess of bestowing importance upon the wearer. Insignificant-looking women, to whom before nobody had paid any attention, now came into notice, and portly women became positively awful in their majesty. One can imagine the effect produced in a country church when the squire's lady appeared for the first time in a hoop—how the farmers' daughters would stare and feel the gulf between them and the "quality" yawning wider and wider; how the school children would be sternly reproved in loud whispers for giggling, and frowned into order by teachers as curious and interested as themselves; and how the old people who depended on the hall for their comforts would drop a rather deeper curtsy as the gentlefolk passed down the path when the service was over.

By the middle of the century the country was following more closely in the wake of the town. "Fifty years ago," says a writer in 1761, "the dress of people in distant counties was no more like those in town than Turkish or Chinese. But now in the course of a tour you will not meet with a high crowned hat or a pair of red stockings." The high-crowned hat was pretty well confined to the Quakers, who were as noticeable for the neatness as for the old-fashioned cut of their garments. Their linen was always fine and clean, and the quality of their sober-coloured coats and gowns was of the best. The most rigid discarded all additions which could in any way be described as ornaments, even to the buttons with which it was the fashion to loop up the hats. The men's hats were lower and wider brimmed than the women's, which were of the regular steeple shape. Quakers, of course, did not wear wigs.

Madame Boccage (referred to in a previous chapter) notes the thriving appearance of the agricultural folk, how well dressed and well housed were the families of farmers and shepherds. She observed that the "poorest country girls had bodices of chintz, straw hats on their heads, and scarlet cloaks on their shoulders." The straw hat was despised by the better classes in the country; they indulged in velvet hoods. Sometimes these hoods were scarlet, as appears from a witty letter to the *Spectator*, signed "Joan and Martha Upstarts." "You must know that I and my sister Martha Upstart are excommunicated from church for appearing there in hoods the same colour as our parson's nose, which, being of the brightest red, we thought it most agreeable to our complexions, having none of that colour in our own faces, though there is not a shade of that sort but appears in our Vicar's. Had it not been our good fortune to wear our hoods first upon a very cold day, we had still been admitted as the genteelest part of his congregation; for the sharpness of our Yorkshire air has that metamorphosing quality, that while he is in his pulpit there appears variety of blues, from the deepest mazarene down to the palest purple, which shades are very much darkened by a settled blackness at the tip of his nose and chin. My milloner, Mary Pert, having been the occasion of our misfortunes, we humbly beg you will punish her by obliging our parson to marry her, we being very well informed he will make the worst of husbands. By this means you may put a stop to their impudently imposing fashions upon us country ladies, who have not been allowed to appear in our own parish church, since the 30th January, King Charles' martyrdom."

Female fashionable attire in the eighteenth century was very ill fitted for country life, which is so largely spent out-of-doors. Indeed, it was not fitted for out-door wear at all. No fashionable woman was properly shod, in the first place, for the coloured shoes which, as has been stated, all ladies wore, were not adapted for vigorous exercise or damp weather with their high heels and very open tops. Those were the kind of shoes worn for walking in London. Country life in shoes of that sort would mean endless expense. The wonder is that town-bred women did not insist upon the shoemakers providing something more fitted for the dirty, uneven pathways. But then walking was not a daily exercise as it is now. Foot-gear has undergone much reformation in the present century, in spite of the persistence of high heels.

In men's dress the same difference was observable. The country squires, "with their triple bands and triple buckles on their hats," who had to be restrained from attending the Bath Assemblies in their heavy boots, were not used to the silk stockings and fine shoes of the town gallants, and looked upon such articles as signs of effeminacy. The male dress of the middle classes in London was pretty much the dress of the middle classes in the country, and of the more old-fashioned country gentlemen. Coats were long and voluminous, with wide skirts, baggy sleeves, and capacious pockets. Waistcoats were long too, so were cravats, and wigs were large and bushy. Plain, broad-brimmed hats of the shovel type were used a good deal in the country, and by the poorer among the commonalty in London, but cocked hats were generally worn. Even the workman had his cocked hat, only it was not laced like his master's. He wore a wig, too, the variety called the bob-wig. His coat was generally well buttoned up, for he had no elegant white shirt to display, and possibly no waistcoat, and his coat cuffs were very long, because there were no ruffles at the wrists. He wore shoes—the universal wear—which came well over the foot, what are described as high-quartered shoes, and coarse worsted stockings. In the country, wigs do not seem to have been worn by the working classes as they were in London.

To the Continentals we seemed a luxurious nation. It was remarked that the very peasants were dressed in cloth. The husbandman, however, wore a coarse linen smock over his cloth. "Even the common people," says one astonished traveller, "have embroidered vests." So they had, for embroidery was much used on cloth then, and waistcoats were seldom made quite plain. It is difficult to credit the accuracy of the same observer when he says, "Nobody, even among the common people, wears a turned coat or a soled shoe. Shirts of the finest linen are generally worn, and even the lower sort have a clean one every day." To turn a coat is not an easy task; it might be better economy to wear it right out than to be at the expense of having it re-made, and all cloth will not admit of turning. But as for soled shoes, they were quite as common as they are now. The remark on the shirts is a still greater puzzle. In what quarter of the kingdom did the commonalty wear fine linen shirts and clean ones every day? How could they have afforded the money for such a stock of the finest linen? and how did they persuade their wives into permitting that seven-fold washing? Probably Sunday was the day on which this writer made all his notes. Never before or since the eighteenth century has any one discovered such delightful facts about the dress of the people of England.

It does not say much for French habits that

Grosley, among his many observations, is so impressed with the extreme cleanliness of the English. Whether we deserved the praise he bestowed upon us is very doubtful. There is evidence to show that a hundred or a hundred and fifty years ago scrupulous cleanliness among men was thought rather a weakness. But Grosley says, "The cleanliness of the English in everything is admirable. Fine linen, clean stockings, a neat hat, and good shoes, distinguish the men of easy circumstances." If people in easy circumstances were to be praised for being clean and tidy in England, what must have been the condition of the lower orders in other countries? The only thing that excited censure was the coat. Rich citizens are said to have gone on 'Change in threadbare coats. Overcoats were very thick and long—wrap-rascals they were called sometimes—for nobody of the sterner sex ventured to carry an umbrella if it rained. So the poet's advice was sound :—

> "Nor should it prove thy less important care,
> To chuse a proper coat for winter's wear.
> Now in thy trunk thy *d'oily* habit fold,
> The silken drugget ill can fence the cold;
> The frieze's spongy nap is soak'd with rain,
> And show'rs soon drench the camlet's cockled grain.
> True Witney broad-cloth with its shag unshorn,
> Unpierc'd is in the lasting tempest worn;
>
> *   *   *   *   *   *

> That garment best the winter's rage defends,
> Which from the shoulders full and low depends;
> By various names in various countries known
> Yet held in all the true surtout alone:
> Be thine of Kersey, firm tho' small the cost.
> Then brave unwet the rain, unchill'd the frost." *

Umbrellas were a recent fashion in the earlier part of the century. During the first ten years of George the Third's reign the only umbrellas in use were large carriage umbrellas, which required an attendant to hold them. In the country they were hardly known at all. The philanthropist, Jonas Hanway, in 1756, boldly unfurled an umbrella in the streets of London, being the first man who ventured upon such an innovation. Surely Hanway deserves to be held in grateful remembrance by the male sex for this spirited effort towards the emancipation of his brethren from the thraldom of custom. He was jeered and ridiculed by the populace, but was not to be laughed into giving up the sheltering oilskin. About twenty years later, a valiant footman, named John Macdonald, began to use a silk umbrella which he had brought from Spain. The boys shouted after him, "Frenchman, why don't you get a coach?" but he grasped his umbrella more firmly and went on his way, and in some three months' time he was able to use it without exciting remark. Miss

* J. Gay, *Trivia*.

Hutton, writing in 1779, from Derbyshire, says, "Mrs. Greaves lent us their umbrella, and a servant to carry it." Miss Hutton's brother was the second person to use an umbrella in Birmingham, a Frenchman being the first.

The town beau when he first carried an umbrella was caricatured in the prints as the rain-beau holding a tiny parasol over his head. A young gentleman once borrowed an umbrella from the mistress of a coffee-house in Cornhill, and, shortly after, the following satirical advertisement appeared in *The Female Tatler*: "The young gentleman belonging to the Custom house, that for fear of rain borrowed the umbrella from Will's Coffee-house in Cornhill, of the *mistress*, is hereby advertised that to be dry from head to foot on the like occasion he shall be welcome to the *maid's* pattens."

An illustration of the want of umbrellas is afforded in one of the caricatures of the period showing a respectable citizen's family returning from Vauxhall in a downpour of rain—the old gentleman with a handkerchief tied over his head to save his wig, and his wife's cardinal on his shoulders to protect his best coat; while the wife herself and her daughters are tripping along in gowns turned up round their waists, and their heads enveloped in coloured handkerchiefs. In 1797 there was only one umbrella in all Cambridge, and that was kept at a shop, and let out, like a sedan chair, by the hour. In London, women carried umbrellas before men had taken to them; but the first umbrellas were heavy awkward machines, made of oilskin or taffeta. Still, in spite of their cumbrous character, women who had to trudge along the streets on rainy days rejoiced in their shelter. With cloak and umbrella they were able to face the dripping roofs and waterspouts, which were as much to be avoided as the rain. To the fashionable lady who only walked in fine weather the one important consideration was the parasol; but it was otherwise with the thrifty citizeness. Great must have been the relief and saving of clothes when the new invention came into use.

> "Good housewives all the winter's rage despise,
> Defended by the riding hood's disguise;
> Or underneath the umbrella's oily shade,
> Safe through the wet on clinking pattens tread.
> Let Persian dames the umbrella's ribs display,
> To guard their beauties from the sunny ray;
> Or sweating slaves support the shady load,
> When Eastern monarchs show their state abroad;
> Britain in winter only knows its aid,
> To guard from chilling showers the walking maid." *

Well-to-do women of the trading class, who lived in the city, imitated, as far as they could, the dress and habits of those who belonged to the

* J. Gay, *Trivia*.

fashionable world. One of their favourite customs was to rise late. "A merchant's wife and not breakfasted before ten! Fye upon you, Dolly! these are new fashions, these are courtly customs; let us stick to the city—old city hours; and the idle jade Loetitia loves her pillow better than she does her prayers."* City madams wore brocaded petticoats and satin gowns, tricked out their hair, and made their head-dresses as large as they could, wore big *buffonts* at the neck, smart shoes, and were very particular about their muffs, fans, and snuff-boxes. An eighteenth-century lady generally had a snuff-box among her appendages. The following lines were penned by a gentleman who borrowed a lady's snuff-box :—

> "Envy'd toy, attend her side;
> Or, beneath her pillow laid,
> Nightly yield thy friendly aid.
> * * * *
> But tell her when she tastes thy treasure,
> Poison's mix'd with every pleasure."

Snuff-taking was as common a habit among all classes as smoking is now. When the lottery passion was rampant in 1753, it was noticed that poor people went without their snuff in order to buy lottery tickets.†

* Cumberland, *The Choleric Man*.   † H. Walpole.

Although a great deal has been written about the prevalence of tight-lacing in the eighteenth century, English women did not sin so deeply in this respect as French women. "Instead of that armour of whalebone, still made use of in France, to put a force upon nature, and which often quite spoils it, they use in England only a sort of whalebone waistcoat which just reaches to the breast, and has no other effect but that of keeping the body in a slight compression. Two ribbands, from the fore to the hind part, keep it on, without bridling or putting any constraint upon the shoulders." This observation must have been made at a time when low stays were being worn. The fashion changed frequently; sometimes they were made very high, compressing the figure a good deal and giving it a very ugly shape. It is pleasant to hear that "a good shape is the most striking article of English beauty, from which it is almost inseparable," for it has often been said that the English lack elegance of form and carriage.

As time went on there was less difference to be observed between the dress of the aristocracy and that of the middle classes. Even early in the century, Misson says that Englishmen dress in a plain, uniform manner. Men who did not affect to be beaux wore quiet cloth suits for everyday wear, and reserved their silk and lace for *fêtes*. It was said to be difficult to distinguish a lord from a plain citizen. But this was partly because the citizen had become more ambitious in his ideas. "Every tradesman is a merchant, every merchant a gentleman, and every gentleman one of the noblesse." Some members of Parliament who professed Republican principles attended the House of Commons without wigs, even without powder on their hair, and clad in dull-coloured common cloth suits. They were not over-particular about cleanliness, and would get up to speak with hands "as black as those of a hatter." These men were not at all like their Republican brethren in France, who were usually rather gay in their attire. "Everybody in summer as well as in winter wears a plain coat, but of the finest cloth; no tradesman will wear anything else. No furs are used, but great surtouts which protect from rain in summer and cold in winter. In this simple dress do the first ministers of the state walk the streets of London without being followed by a single servant."

Among the women the fashions adopted by the richer classes were eagerly copied by the poorer, as in modern days. The train was the great temptation of all women. Those who could not afford to renew their clothes frequently, preferred a draggled tail to none at all. There were many "who would have a tail though they wanted a petticoat, and others who, without any other pretensions, fancied they became ladies merely from the addition of three superfluous yards of silk." The women of the commonalty who did not indulge in hoops and trains wore gowns with full round pleated skirts, sleeves large at the top, and tightly fitting bodices. Their hats were broad-brimmed, and not unlike the men's, only the crowns were lower, and they wore caps underneath, tied at the chin. Instead of hats and caps they sometimes wore large bonnets that came well over the ears and the back of the head. In bad weather they put on pattens which lifted them out of the mud, and in which they were able to trudge along the dirty streets with comparatively little damage to their clothes.

There were numerous callings, the members of which had their distinctive dress. One of the best-known characters of old London was the watchman who disturbed people quietly asleep in their beds with his cries and tramping, which gave ample notice to evil-doers of his approach. But the watchman, if he were an insufficient guardian of the peace, was useful as a guide to belated roisterers, whose conviviality was likely to land them in the gutter.

> "Yet there are watchmen who, with friendly light,
> Will teach thy reeling steps to tread aright;
> For sixpence, will support thy helpless arm,
> And home conduct thee safe from nightly harm."

The London watchman was certainly not clad with a view to pursuing agile thieves or other lawbreakers. He was wrapped in a wide-skirted heavy coat, a useful garment for protecting him from the cold, but not adapted to enable him to cope with the bullies who assaulted the weak and unprotected. He wore low shoes and a big broad-brimmed hat, which could be turned up or down, worn forward or backward. The only means of defence which the watchman seems to have possessed was a staff something like a beadle's. In his left hand he carried his lantern.

The hackney coachman, who, at first, did not sit upon the box but upon the horse, was not attired much more suitably. He wore a loose coat with turn-down collar; a broad-brimmed hat, in the rim of which the rain gathered and dripped down upon his shoulders, unprotected by any cape; and baggy trousers, stuffed into broad-topped boots, which would have kept the wet out better if the tops had been turned up instead of down. As long as he continued to ride he wore spurs. Among the numerous dealers and hawkers was the rat-catcher, whose costume was similar to that of the hackney coachman, though doubtless the latter would have felt indignant at the comparison. But the rat-catcher in a coat with turn-down collar, baggy trousers, and broad-brimmed hat, had much the same appearance as the coachman, except that his coat was shorter and tighter.

A notable itinerant trader of the middle of the eighteenth century, known to all Londoners, was William Conway, of Bethnal Green, who made a living by selling and exchanging metal spoons. As he walked twenty-five miles a day, Sundays excepted, his shoes were the most important articles of his attire, and these he made out of the uppers of old boots. A pair of shoes lasted him six weeks. He was an odd figure, with his long spindle legs encased in tight knee-breeches, short coat, high hat, and bag slung over his shoulder.*

Then there were the men who went about the streets playing odd music on odder instruments, and who affected a jaunty style of dress, wore coats quite short in the front, very tightly fitting pantaloons and shoes. The ballad-man was much less smart in his appearance, more like a street hawker of to-day, except that his ill-fitting trousers were buttoned up the leg.

* J. T. Smith, *Cries of London.*

Numbers of chairmen, porters, and gentlemen's servants were always about the streets, recognizable at a glance by trifling peculiarities in their costume. Servants usually wore livery. The footman with his high, cocked hat, and coat with deep cape, swaggered along with an insolent air, and was not at all a pleasant person to encounter in a narrow, crowded thoroughfare.

> "Yet who the footman's arrogance can quell,
> Whose flambeau gilds the sashes of Pall Mall,
> When in long rank a train of torches flame
> To light the midnight visits of the dame?"

The shoeblack cleaned his customers' shoes in a coat with skirts as long as those of his patrons, and which spread all round him as he bent over his block, brush in hand. He was as well known a figure in eighteenth-century London as he is to-day. "Clean your honour's shoes?" resounded in all the principal streets.

> "Hark! the boy calls thee to his destin'd stand,
> And the shoe shines beneath his oily hand."

The milkmaids were quite one of the sights of London, on May-day, in their yellow and red quilted petticoats, pink and blue gowns, mob caps with lace lappets, and flat straw hats trimmed with ribbons, named after Peg Woffington. During their revels they were attended by fiddlers in sky-blue coats and hats covered with ribbons.

A glance at the picture of a young shopman with his wig carefully tied, his ruffles in good order, and his big bow of black ribbon at his throat, does not reveal much difference of attire from that of the gentlemen customers. Outward equality caused many complaints in the eighteenth century. It was an age which scouted the notion that a tradesman could by any possibility be a gentleman. The *Tatler*, writing in the character of a sober trader who knows his place and likes to keep it, says that he beheld with no small concern, in " coffee houses and public places, my brethren, the tradesmen of this city, put off the smooth, even, and ancient decorum of thriving citizens for a fantastical dress and figure improper for their persons and characters, to the utter destruction of that order and distinction which of right ought to be between St. James's and Milk Street, the Camp and Cheapside. I have given myself some time to find out how distinguishing the frays in a lot of muslins, or drawing up a regiment of thread laces, or making a panegyric on pieces of sagathy or Scotch plaid should entitle a man to a laced hat or sword, a wig tied up with ribbons, or an embroidered coat. The college say this enormity proceeds from a sort of delirium in the brain, which makes it break out at first about the head, and for want of timely remedies falls upon the left thigh, and from thence in little ways and windings, run over the whole body, as appears by pretty ornaments on the buttons, button-holes, garterings, sides of the breeches and the like."

CHAPTER IX.

Trade and commerce—The silk trade—Lustrings and *à la mode* silks—Smuggling—Prohibition against wearing of Indian calicoes—Lace smuggled in large quantities—The linen trade—Cotton—New machines—The woollen trade—Prosperity of Norwich—The glove trade—The policy of protection.

"The single dress of a woman of quality is often the product of a hundred climates. The muff and the fan come together from the different ends of the earth. The scarf is sent from the torrid zone, and the tippet from beneath the pole. The brocade petticoat rises out of the mines of Peru, and the diamond necklace out of the bowels of Indostan."—ADDISON, *Benefits of Commerce.*

How far trade affects fashion, and how far fashion affects trade, is a nice question for economists. Both trade and fashion are swayed, independently of their interaction on each other, by outside matters—by politics, by the personal preferences of sovereigns, by increased facilities for inter-communication, by the spread of education, by discoveries and inventions. A political event that greatly affected one branch of trade at the end of the seventeenth century has already been noted, viz. the settlement in England of large numbers of skilled silk-throwers, driven from France by religious persecution. Our silk-manufactures were then in a very backward state. England depended almost wholly on foreign markets for her supplies, importing silk goods annually to the value of £600,000 or £700,000. In 1692 the French refugees settled in Spitalfields, who, for some half-dozen years, had been industriously carrying on the manufacture of different kinds of silk not made, or very imperfectly made, in England before, obtained a patent for the sole right of making the two sorts of silk most in vogue then, viz. lustrings and *à la mode* silk, which had hitherto been brought from France. Again, in 1711, the silk-weavers petitioned that means might be found to keep the manufacture in England free from the interference of French traders, whose action had so hampered the business of the Lustring Company that the number of looms had been reduced from 768 to 100.

The Spitalfields workers, among whom were, of course, English operatives, persuaded Parliament to pass an Act prohibiting the importation of all foreign silks except those from India and China. That would be a large exception now, but at that period most of our silks came from France. The loss to the French trade was great, although French silks did not cease to be worn in England, for they were smuggled over at the rate of £500,000 per annum. In 1719 an Englishman, who had studied the machinery for silk-throwing in Italy, obtained a patent, and set up a mill on the Derwent, where he carried on the manufacture with success. This enterprise of John Lombe was the next important step in the development of the English silk trade.

The war with France which followed the settlement of the French refugees, materially affected English trade and manufactures. Commercial intercourse between the two countries being stopped, England had to look elsewhere for those things which France had been in the habit of supplying. For the coarse linens which had been imported from Brittany and other parts we turned to Hamburg, and our own hat trade received an impetus when the cheap felt hats made in Normandy could no longer be imported. English merchants took great exception to the commercial treaty proposed at the Peace of Utrecht in 1713, and succeeded in making Parliament refuse assent to the articles reducing the duties and removing the prohibitions on French commodities. War again broke out in the reign of George II., and throughout the century embroilments recurred which interfered with, and sometimes entirely prevented, all legitimate trade with France. But in the eighteenth century, as in former periods, the taste for foreign stuffs—especially French stuffs—in the fashionable world was very decided, and, although all our sovereigns showed a patriotic desire to encourage English manufactures, the nobility and well-to-do classes were far from imitating their example.

In 1719 Steele tried to enlist public sympathy on behalf of the English woollen manufactures, by publishing an essay written to show what a large proportion of the garments worn by the richer classes were of foreign make. "I shall take the modern English lady at eleven o'clock in the forenoon, which is her break of day, and allowing her to twelve for private devotion, suppose she has called to be dressed, and from the parcels of her dress observing what she wears of English and what of foreign product, with the prices of each part of her habit, make my inferences accordingly. None amongst those whom we call people of condition can be at home or abroad, visit or receive visits, without having several dresses with several suitable undresses, according to the following list of absolute necessaries for a fine lady." Then come numerous items of dress all priced, including a cambric Holland smock, a Marseilles quilted petticoat, a French or Italian silk quilted petticoat, a French point or Flanders laced "head," two

French hoods, French gloves and flowers, and an Italian fan; only two articles appear to be English, viz. the silk stockings and the stays; the sum-total comes to £210 7s. 6d.

Steele goes on to say: "This is the necessary demand upon every gentleman, who would live in the fashion and in quiet, for one dress for his lady; and as it would be scandalous (as his wife, anxious for his reputation, according to her duty, admonishes him) for her to be known by her cloathes, she cannot but have five suits at least, and even with that she must stay at home one day in the week. . . . According to this rule, foreigners sell this lady to the value of a thousand pounds, where the English sell her to the value of five, and I believe any company or person, trade or trader, on the British side of the Channel, will find it hard to balance this loss to our country by what they sell of English cloathing to foreigners. I shall not, therefore, press the advantage further in the argument, so far as to mention that her garters are French, and cost one pound five; that she has a pair of pockets of Marseilles quilting, which is another one pound five. . . . I had like to have concluded without taking notice that the lining of her gown and petticoat was Italian lute-string, cheap at eight pounds; but on the English side of the account which I forgot when about her legs, it must be added that she had thread stockings, worth ten shillings. . . . The cap on which her head is dressed is foreign silk, and so is the lace that ties it, as well as the lace for the stays. But for our encouragement at home, we supply her with pins, patches, powder, and wire. Patches may perhaps make a fraction in the account, therefore it must be considered that it is English labour upon Italian silk. I am dressing her for a visit; and as she is going out, she calls for her Turkey handkerchief, for which she gave five guineas. . . . The apartments through which I am to conduct this lady are hung with foreign silks, and the chairs covered with the same." *

The influence of fashion on certain commodities was very marked. All through the century there was a market for the lustrings made by the Spitalfields weavers. Lustring seems to have been an expensive silk used for *fête* dresses. Mrs. Delany speaks of having a gown in which to attend a wedding, made of brocaded lustring (spelt also lutestring). It was white, with "great ramping flowers in shades of purples, reds, and greens." She adds, quite unnecessarily, that "it will make a great show." This lustring cost thirteen shillings a yard, but plain lustring could be had for half that

* Steele, *The Spinster.*

price. Another lady appeared on the same occasion in a lustring brocaded with silver and flowers. It is one of the materials that has vanished with the century, like the *à la mode* silks,—at least under those names. To encourage the manufacture of *à la mode* silk, the Court and nobility took to wearing it for mourning hat-bands at one time, instead of the crape which Sir Robert Walpole had introduced into Court mourning. Rigid Protestants objected to crape, because it was made in Italy. Another silk that we have lost now, but which was used in the last century, was shagreen. It was a much cheaper silk than lustring, and more resembled taffeta, not having such a smooth surface as silk. A good shagreen could be had for four shillings a yard.

Towards the close of the reign of Queen Anne the manufacture of silk in England had greatly increased, and our goods were able to bear comparison with those manufactured in France, thanks to the short-sighted policy which sent us instructors from that country. A great many silk hoods were worn, and material for these was made to the value of £300,000 yearly. During the first twenty years of the century the silk trade made a great stride, and George I., to encourage the manufacture of English silk fabrics, granted bounties on their exportation. The raw material came from the East, from the Levant, from Persia and China, and from time to time facilities were afforded for its importation by reducing the duties. The East India Company, and next to them the Russian Company, were the two great importers of raw silk, carrying English wool in exchange. The French began to compete with us in the East India trade, but the English Company kept ahead, and in 1730, when the French Company only had four ships sailing from India, the English Company had seventeen.* In that same year, we find raw silk exported from England, together with thrown silk, and our manufactured goods found a ready sale even in Italy, where English silk stockings were highly esteemed. In the reign of George II., in order to encourage the culture of raw silk in the English colonies in America, an Act was passed admitting the products of the colonies duty free. In South Carolina and Georgia the production of raw silk greatly increased towards the end of the reign of George II.

But foreign wrought silk continued to be imported, to the indignation of the English silk-workers, who began to be very loud in their complaints, and a certain class of manufactured goods was prohibited. In 1763 a detachment of Guards

* Anderson, *Origin of Commerce.*

had to be quartered in Spitalfields in order to suppress the riots of the journeymen weavers, the master silk-weavers petitioning for the aid of the military. These riots arose out of a dispute about wages. The journeymen demanded an increase, and, on being refused, they assembled to the number of two thousand, masked and disguised, and armed with cutlasses and other weapons. They then proceeded to the houses of those journeymen who had refused to combine with them, broke their looms, and committed various outrages. In the year 1765 the weavers marched in procession from Spitalfields to Westminster, carrying flags made of French silk, and, after a conference at the Guildhall, the mercers and masters agreed to recall all contracts for foreign goods.

Although at this time silk stockings were well made in England, they were constantly smuggled from abroad with more or less success. Nobody was above using contraband articles, and it was common for people to ask their friends when they went on the Continent to bring or send back goods that were either prohibited altogether, or on which heavy duties were levied. In 1765 the Honourable Henry St. John asks George Selwyn to order for him twelve pairs of silk stockings, eight of the finest white silk, and four of light grey.

There would be no difficulty, he explained, about passing them if they were washed and marked. The Earl of March tells Selwyn that all his stockings had been seized through the want of taking the precaution of rolling them up like old stockings.

The influence which trade could exercise over fashion was seen at the end of the seventeenth century—when the East India Company flooded the market with India chintzes and calicoes. English manufacturers became so alarmed, and home industries were thought to be in such danger, that in 1701 an Act was passed by which all printed calicoes, wrought silks, and other stuffs from India, Persia, and China, were locked up, on arrival, in warehouses until they could be exported, and no one was permitted to use such goods in England under a penalty of two hundred pounds. It was the printed calicoes, above all, that were so popular; there was nothing made in England to equal them, the cotton and calico trade not being then developed. The importation was carried on secretly, until, in 1719, the Spitalfields weavers rose in revolt, and went about the streets assaulting every one they met wearing an Indian calico. George I., like Anne, was desirous of encouraging both the silk and woollen manufactures, and prohibited the use of Indian stuffs, the penalty being five pounds for each offence on the wearer, and twenty pounds on the seller. Another Act was passed at the same time against the using of cloth for buttons and button-holes, that the consumption of raw silk and mohair yarn might be increased.

Between 1719 and 1720 Steele took up the cudgels for the weavers in the Eastern counties, and wrote an article entitled "The Female Manufacturers' Complaint," wherein it was affirmed that yarn could no longer find a sale either in Norwich or London, that "many woollen stuffs mixed with silk, and even silks themselves, are in a very great measure laid aside, that some of them are quite lost, and thrown out of sale, such as brilliants and pulerays, antherines and bombazines, satinets and chiverets, oraguellas, grazetts, a great variety of silk and worsted footworks, flowered grazetts, flowered silk and worsted tammy draughts and damasks, fine coloured crapes. . . . This sudden change, which is apparently to the ruin of many thousands of your petitioners, is brought about in favour of a tawdry, pie-spotted, flabby, ragged, low-priced thing, called callicoe; a foreigner by birth; made the Lord knows where, by a parcel of heathens and pagans, that worship the devil and work for a halfpenny a day. . . . As the general wearing of callicoes is the complaint, the general leaving them off will be the cure. The fashion is the grievance, because it is a fashion; it is in the ladies' power at once to make it odious and abhorred all over the kingdom. . . . If the women in England will but set their hands to this work, not a callicoe, not a piece of linen printed or stained, shall be sold in England."*

Although sumptuary laws had long ceased to be enacted, the Government, in the last century, were constantly interfering with costume by forbidding certain foreign stuffs to be used when they wanted to develop a home industry. An instance of this occurred in 1747, when large kerchiefs of fine white French cambric were worn folded round the shoulders. An outcry was raised against the importation of French lawn or cambric, and an Act was accordingly passed prohibiting its use, and imposing a penalty of five pounds on every one detected in using the forbidden material in any way about their dress.

Of course quantities of lace were smuggled, for the fashionable world was clothed in lace, and preferred the fine Flemish lace to that made in England, good as it was,—for the lace industry, thanks again to foreign refugees, had greatly developed. People evaded the duties in every

* Steele, *Town Talk.*

possible way, women being specially ingenious in escaping the Custom House officers. Lace shirts and ruffles were put into coffins and passed as corpses, but the trick was practised so often that the authorities grew suspicious of coffins. Lace was often stuffed in with the dead body. The High Sheriff of Westminster found six thousand pounds' worth of French lace in the coffin of Dr. Atterbury, who died in Paris in 1731. There were angry expostulations on the part of English manufacturers about the use of foreign lace. Queen Anne had forbidden gold and silver lace—for which there was much demand—to be brought in at all, but no edicts availed against the passion for lace. At the wedding of Frederick Prince of Wales, in 1736, there was a great display of patriotism among the bridal party; the bride and bridegroom both wore lace of English make, the bridal robe being of the handsomest lace England could produce, and nearly all the guests patronized the home manufactures. A society was started, called the Anti-Gallicans, to uphold the home industry and distribute prizes to the workers.

When George III. came to the throne he at once showed his desire to stem the tide of importation. In 1764 the King's sister, Princess Augusta, was married to the Duke of Brunswick, and an order was issued that not only all the lace, but all materials worn at the wedding, were to be of English make. But the invited company gave no heed to the royal command, with the result that, three days before the marriage, the Custom House officer paid a visit to the Court milliner, and finding her establishment stocked with garments of foreign make, carried them all off.* How the despoiled ladies and gentlemen contrived fresh toilets history does not record. A bale of French lace, to the weight of nearly one hundred pounds, was also seized and burnt in that same year. But smuggling still went on, and three years later another seizure of lace was made, to the value of four hundred pounds. Such heavy duties were laid upon foreign lace that the utmost vigilance of the Custom House officers could not stop the illicit trade.

There was a general feeling in favour of foreign goods of all sorts among the well-to-do classes. "I have seen a lady dressed from top to toe in her own manufactures formerly. But nowadays, there's nothing of their own manufacture about them except their own faces."† A great deal of satin, damask, and velvet was used by the wealthy, and nearly all of this came from abroad. Velvet was smuggled like lace. "The pattern of

* Palliser, *History of Lace*.   † *The Good Natured Man.*

velvet you sent me," writes Gilly Williams to George Selwyn, in 1784, "is so pretty that it has made me alter my intentions, and determines me to risk the vigilance of the Custom House officers." People were resolved to have their foreign silks and velvets at any cost.

How the rise of certain fashions affected trade may be seen in the great demand for damask at the time when large hoops were worn. There was nothing that looked so well over a large hoop—if anything made in that way could look well—as a rich damask. Its silky, flowered surface, not being gathered into folds, but stretched out tightly, showed to the best advantage. Damask is a heavy material, but wearers of hoops did not regard the weight of their clothes. "The fashionable hoops," writes Mrs. Delany, in 1738, "are made of the richest damask, trimmed with gold and silver, fourteen guineas a hoop." The price of damask varied from seven to fourteen shillings a yard. On another occasion Mrs. Delany speaks of having bought "a scarlet damask manteau and petticoat," so the use of damask was not confined to hoops. In descriptions of Court costume and fashionable dress generally there is constant mention of damask petticoats. Velvet was also used for petticoats, though not so much as damask; but there was plenty of demand for velvet for turbans, and the large Rubens and Devonshire hats.

The style of dress which prevailed during the greater part of the century brought in the use of stiff materials. All the female part of the fashionable world wanted rich, solid damasks, velvets, satins, and silks. It was not until towards the end of the century that the lighter make of goods, like crapes and muslins, became popular. And in gentlemen's dress it was much the same. All sorts of fancy velvets and flowered satins were in request. It being a period when every woman, young or old, wore a head-dress, there was always a sale for the smaller silken goods, such as ribbons, and for feathers, flowers, and gauze. By-and-by the fashion changed, and white and coloured crapes, spangled and embroidered, took the place of damasks and satins.

During the last decade of the century a rage for muslins set in, and women of the upper classes were all walking, dining, and dancing in muslins. The whole style of dress changed. Clinging gowns pushed out the heavy damasks and brocades, and in 1784 the only silks used were thin soft silks like Persian, which was a cheap material compared with damask, averaging about one shilling and eightpence a yard. The use of muslin, though it must have affected the silk trade for a time, did not make so much difference in the sum-total spent upon clothing, for good book muslin fetched seven shillings a yard, and other clear muslins four and sixpence, and their durability was very inferior to that of silk goods.

Although wool was the staple trade of England, woollen underclothing was practically unknown. The commonalty may have used a rough woollen material for shirts, but more generally the cheap, coarse linens. Among the richer classes there was always a large supply wanted of the finest linen Holland could produce for shirts and ladies' smocks. There was also a great deal of fine damask used for table-linen. The English linen trade was in a precarious condition, and had to be propped up with protective enactments. As William and Mary did a good deal to encourage the home linen trade, it is interesting to glance at some of the items in the royal household accounts relative to linen. A total of £700 a year was spent on the linen provided for the tables of the King and Queen, who had separate accounts. The washing of this linen was put down at £200 a year. The laundress who washed the body linen of the King and Queen was paid nearly £220 a year, and upwards of £180 for the expenses of the laundry and materials.*

* *Publications of the Society of Antiquaries.*

There was a great difference in the price of British and foreign linen. A shirt made of good Scotch or Irish linen could be had for seven and sixpence, while the shirts made of Holland linen ran up to a guinea. As the usual price paid for the linen sheets supplied to the royal household was from three to four shillings an ell, most of it was probably of home manufacture. The duty on exported linen was taken off in 1711; it was made a penal offence in 1721 to sell or weave calicoes unless the warp were wholly of linen.* In 1722 a woman was actually seized in the City for wearing a gown faced with calico, and committed to the Compter as she refused to pay the fine.† In 1746 the British Linen Company was started; and to promote the manufacture of sail-cloth, all ships were required on their first sailing to be provided with English sail-cloth. This enactment applied as well to ships built in the British Colonies.

The British Linen Company was incorporated in 1764, with the special object of making cambrics and lawns to take the place of the prohibited French goods. In 1765 a Bill was passed for "the better establishing a manufactory of cambricks and lawns at Winchelsea," and generally for promoting the

* A. J. Warden, *History of the Linen Trade.*
† *Ibid.*

trade throughout the country. Winchelsea was chosen as the centre for the manufacture of these imitation goods, because it was into that port that French goods were often smuggled. All cambrics made by the British Linen Company were exported duty free to the American colonies. In 1767 the duties on imported linen were increased.

The manufacture of Irish linen was meantime much increasing. In 1741 the export was one hundred times as great as it was fifty years previously.* There was a good deal of linen spun in Scotland, too, in the first half of the eighteenth century, when the making of linen was quite a domestic industry. Scotch linen was about one-third of the price of linen from Holland. But both the English and Scotch linen trade declined from various causes between 1770 and 1773, and subsequently the growth of the cotton manufacture in England affected the linen trade.

The English cotton trade was developed by the genius of four inventors—John Kay with his fly shuttle, James Hargreaves with his spinning jenny, Samuel Crompton with the mule, and Richard Arkwright with the spinning frame. It was not until Arkwright's invention that a piece of pure cotton cloth was made in England. Cotton goods began

* A. J. Warden, *History of the Linen Trade.*

to be used in place of printed linens for gowns. As far as underclothing went the linen trade was secure, for cotton goods were not substituted for linen until a much later period. But printed cottons, like the printed calicoes from India, came very much into use. At a Welsh wedding in 1797 we read of cotton gowns being worn by the ladies who came from towns, while those who came from mountainous districts were clad in woollen.* Both cottons and muslins were made in such quantities by the English looms, that in 1793 the East India Company complained of the injury to their imports. Every shop was selling British muslins. It was Crompton's spinning mule that enabled the yarn to be made fine as well as firm, and caused the muslins imported from India to be successfully imitated by English manufacturers.

In the middle of the century there were complaints rife about the decline of British commerce. "The real source of the decline," says a correspondent to *The London Magazine*, writing from Brabant in 1767, "is in a great measure owing to the secret agents employed in England, who induce our artificers, etc., to go and settle themselves abroad. .... I have seen with great concern upon the spot where I am at present several deluded English

* *Reminiscences of a Gentlewoman of the Last Century.*

artists of various trades pass through the country where I am, with their children, to go and settle themselves in foreign parts."

Yet at this time the woollen industry was in a flourishing condition. Norwich was at the height of its prosperity. It was the leading city in England for the production of woollen goods. The finishing processes that could not be carried out in other places were accomplished in Norwich, which received goods from various parts of the country to be dyed and pressed. Between 1730 and 1760 Norwich had, on an average, twelve thousand looms at work, and fifteen thousand persons engaged in the cloth trade. The best weavers earned from fourteen to twenty-one shillings a week, the women's wages being nearly equal to those of the men, and children were employed at from half a crown to three and sixpence per week. A large variety of goods was produced at Norwich, such as bombazines, camlets, crapes, serges, poplins, and grenadines, besides many things that have passed out of use, like rosettas and russalines. A good deal of the Norwich manufactures found their way abroad until the Thirty Years' War put a check on the export trade to the Continent. Then came the rise of the northern counties—of Yorkshire in particular. In 1773 Bradford had taken a start, and the Yorkshire men and the Norfolk men were in constant rivalry.

There were other parts of England besides the east and north where the wool trade was actively carried on. Exeter exported upwards of 330,000 pieces of cloth in 1768, and at Wellington, Barnstaple, Tiverton, Bath, and other West of England cities and towns there were flannels, serges, and druggets made in considerable quantities. In 1790 there were a thousand looms in Tiverton, and two hundred wool-combers.* Some difficulty was experienced early in the century in ascertaining the exact amount of the exports, as, after the duties on woollen goods were taken off, the merchants, for reasons of their own, were in the habit of entering larger amounts than were actually exported.

Among the lesser trades the glove industry deserves mention, for gloves were as important a feature of dress in the last century as now. In the reign of George III. an Act was passed which empowered the Custom House officers to seize all gloves coming from abroad. Before this a penalty of twenty pounds had been inflicted on persons who imported gloves beyond the quantity required for personal use, but this was not deemed sufficient

* J. Bonwick, *Romance of the Wool Trade*.

to protect the glove trade from foreign competition. An ingenious mode of eluding the Act was sometimes successfully carried out. Gloves would be sent over in two packets, one all for the right hand, the other all for the left. If they escaped detection, well and good; while if one of the lots were seized and put up for auction—which was the usual way of disposing of illicit imports—the owner could buy in his property for next to nothing, as gloves for one hand were of course valueless to any one but the owner of the corresponding lot.* The year 1785, which saw fresh taxes put upon a great many articles, introduced a glove tax, varying according to the price of the gloves from one penny to threepence per pair. Pitt estimated that the tax would yield fifty thousand pounds per annum, but it did not fulfil his expectations, and, after a trial of nine years, was repealed.

Protection was the keynote of commercial life in the last century. Jealousy of the "foreigner" was strong among all ranks in the trading class. If any branch of industry slackened, the cry was immediately raised that British manufactures were suffering from the presence of French, Spanish, or Eastern goods, and heavy duties were levied on certain imports, or they were prohibited entrance

* W. S. Beck, *The Glove Trade*.

altogether. Efforts were constantly being made to promote English trade by artificial means, by bounties, by attempts to foist one class of goods upon the market and exclude others, which only resulted in people obtaining illicitly what they were prevented from getting by fair means. Any method that promised to keep up prices and secure a temporary prosperity for the manufacturing classes was eagerly embraced. Inventions were howled down by the operatives, who regarded a new machine, that would facilitate work, with much the same feeling as they would have regarded a French man-of-war sailing up the Thames. Frequent wars, and the constant apprehension of disturbances, also militated against the interests of commerce. But looking back to the time of the Stuarts, we see how real had been the progress, and how great the gains, insignificant as the sum-total appears now with our enormously multiplied powers and resources.

NINETEENTH CENTURY.

CHAPTER I.

1800–1830.

Rise of the Empire modes—Some eccentricities of costume—Influence of politics on dress—Fanciful costumes—Fashions after the fall of the Empire—Growing plainness in male attire

> "New customs,
> Though they be never so ridiculous
> . . . yet are followed."
>   *Henry VIII.*, Act i. sc. 3.

THE opening of the Nineteenth Century found us still with the long, clinging gowns which had succeeded to the hoop-petticoat. For some years there was very little change. England was under the influence of the classic revival which began in France in the latter part of the eighteenth century. What is known as the Empire mode was evolved out of the modes of the Republic and the Consulate. The same features appear in all three: the short waist, the flowing draperies, the absence of pressure on any part of the figure. The chief difference to be seen between the Empire and the preceding fashions is that there was more richness and elaboration in the costume of the former. Napoleon determined that his Court should be magnificent, should outshine the other Courts of Europe, and he directly encouraged ostentation and extravagance. "Madame la Maréchale," he said one day to a lady, "your cloak is superb; I have seen it a good many times."

We had in England an Anglicized copy of the French imitation of the antique, and reflected the styles of our neighbours in a modified, and, in many respects, improved fashion. There was a good deal of grace about the costumes of these early years of our century. It was their extreme simplicity that gave them their charm. There were no flounces and furbelows, no useless bunched-up drapery; the gown fell in simple straight folds from the neck to the feet, extending into a train of moderate length. The waists were, it is true, unduly short; indeed, the real waist was not seen at all, for the gown only defined the figure a little below the armpits, where there was a girdle composed of a narrow cord and tassels. The neck of the gown was cut low and round, completely covering the shoulders, and the sleeves were short. The success of such a costume depended on the possession of rounded arms, a well-shaped, tapering throat, and an easy, supple bearing. For the women with large elbows, short necks, and thick-set figures Fashion did not provide—she never does; they are left to make the best or the worst of their deficiencies without any kindly aid from the capricious dame, who prefers to suit her modes to the young and well-favoured. This was especially the case when the century was in its teens, frolicking in white muslin morning, noon, and night, spring, summer, autumn, and winter. It was the same in Paris, where Indian muslin was esteemed more than any other material, and was worn by women of all ages; but the French tired of muslins sooner than we did, and went back to their satins and silks for full dress.

Linen and gingham gowns with long trains were worn by the Parisians, who, in their adoration of simplicity, took back into favour the discarded white aprons, which, in England, a few years later, found their way again into full dress. For headgear nothing was so fashionable in Paris as straw hats, which were thought to give a rustic, shepherdess-like character to the costume. Straw hats were very much worn in England, too, especially the gipsy hat tied down with a silk handkerchief. But straw was only worn with morning dress. The time of year mattered nothing. Straw hats were worn in the dull, wintry days as much as in bright sunny weather. For full dress, however, whatever the season, satin hats—generally white—were the mode. A black velvet hat with white feathers might be worn at the opera, but satin was the correct accompaniment to a ball costume. It must be remembered that in those days ladies still danced and dined and appeared at evening parties in hats just as they carried muffs when they were in full evening dress. The muffs for full dress were white. Evening hats, or, as they were called, "dress hats," always had feathers, scarlet being very popular one season. We were not at all insular in our custom of wearing hats indoors; it was quite a Parisian fashion.

But the turban is the most characteristic head-gear of the early nineteenth century. It outlasted many changes in the rest of the costume, and under various shapes, continued in vogue, in spite of the competition of other head-gear. Turbans were of silk, velvet, muslin, lace, and crape, trimmed with flowers, feathers, and ribbons. Girls wore turbans as well as their mothers; it was not until the century had passed its first quarter that turbans were relegated to the use of the more old-fashioned matrons. Turbans were all sorts of shapes and sizes: a piece of lace wound about the head in folds was called a turban as well as the heavy, elaborate confection in velvet and satin. White turbans were much worn by the younger women, the soft crape and muslin of which they were composed making a pretty setting for the face. Our fore-mothers had their afternoon as well as their morning and evening costumes, and white turbans were much used with the afternoon gowns, which, by the way, were much more like evening than day gowns. Gradually the turban was merged into the cap, and we lose sight of it altogether.

There were eccentric features about costume at this period. As in the last century, a marvellous indifference was shown concerning weather. A muslin gown and velvet shoes are prescribed as a suitable walking costume for February, 1803. Who would think of promenading in that guise in February, 1893? And again, in December of that year, cambric muslins were much worn for morning dresses. The evening muslins were either plain book-muslin, or spangled with silver. No wonder that the pelisse figures so largely in the costume of this period. Who could have faced the winter winds in cambric muslin without the protection of the comfortable, enveloping pelisse? It was a long-enduring fashion, resisting all efforts of the cloak, the spencer, and the cape to oust it from its place.

The women of the last generation all wore pelisses. It is only in quite modern days that it has been relegated to the nursery. But the baby's out-door frock and cape is not at all like the original pelisse. It was more like our three-quarter length jacket—the sleeves close and plain, the neck, cuffs, and bottom edged with fur; for the pelisse was more of a winter than a summer garment. It was made of velvet, silk, satin, and sarcenet, a material much in vogue for turbans and gowns. Very bright, startling colours were used for pelisses, such as scarlet, yellow, flame-colour, light blue, pink, and green. And as large glittering buttons were used then, it is quite natural to find the pelisses fastened with gilt and silver buttons.

Light, delicate colours were worn in winter with a complete disregard of the sooty fogs which were common in London. A lady of fashion would be seen walking out in November in an azure-blue sarcenet pelisse elegantly trimmed with ermine, and a Leghorn straw bonnet with blue ribbon bows and a great tuft of white feathers. There were, however, sensible dark cloth pelisses bordered with wide fur, looking very rich and warm. When the Princess of Wales left England for the Continent, in August, 1814, she travelled attired in a dark cloth pelisse fastened with gold clasps. These cloth pelisses, and many of the silk ones too, completely covered the dress, which was a great advantage considering that the morning gown was so commonly of white muslin. What a glorious time it must have been for starchers and ironers and the whole washing sisterhood! Think of the number of white muslin gowns that would be soiled during a week of "London particulars"! The only discoverable merit about walking-dresses is that the skirts were short and the sleeves long. Short sleeves went out of fashion for morning dress after 1807. Trains were reserved for evening wear, and the round muslin robe, which figures so largely in descriptions of morning costume, was made to clear the ground.

Besides the pelisse there were cloaks, long and flowing, which were much worn for driving and at the opera. There were the Prussian blue velvet cloaks, and the Spanish and Cossack cloaks in all colours and materials. Some were extremely elegant, and far more becoming than the high-shouldered cloaks worn recently. For summer there were short cloaks, and mantles something like modern dolmans, long silk scarfs carelessly wound about the neck, and the ever-popular spencers. These were of different styles; some were complete bodices shaped like a blouse, or were open in front like a Zouave; others were quite small, not much more than a handkerchief; they were all short, never going below the waist. A brightly coloured silk spencer worn over a muslin gown made a very smart costume. They were in all colours to please the fancy of the wearer. In 1814 spencers were made with full sleeves and high stand-up collars. A fashionable spencer for hot July weather would be of coloured crape. Morning dresses were usually high; if cut low in the neck, the space was filled up with a kerchief or a ruff.

Early in the century ruffs of a moderate size came in—not the big, Elizabethan ruffs—the low-necked gowns being found so cold in winter. In 1807 ruffs were considered an indispensable addition to morning gowns. They were made of broad lace gathered into a band the size of the throat, and mounted on muslin. Evening gowns were all low in the neck, but if cut very low a fold of muslin or crape, called the half handkerchief, was worn, crossed in front.

The influence of political affairs is seen in the names given to different articles of dress. In 1806 there was a Mameluke robe with a slate-coloured Delta trimming—a reminder of the war in Egypt; the hair was worn *à l'Égyptienne*, that is, adorned with all sorts of jewels, and two rows of beads round the forehead. After the Battle of Austerlitz a nankeen-coloured sarcenet robe trimmed with blue, called the "Austerlitz," was very fashionable. The appellations given to costume were all-embracing. There were Tyrolean and Patmos caps, Turkish embroidery, Pyrenean robes with Etruscan borders, and Arabesque ornaments, and Spanish dresses *à la Paisanne*. There was a great liking for fancy dress in Paris, and English belles also loved to give a foreign air as well as a foreign name to their costumes, to twist their turbans *à la Turque*, or to don a Valencia cloak made with a hood to resemble the cowl of the Order of St. Dominic. The Patmos cap, it may be mentioned, was only worn by the extreme among the *élégantes* and for full dress, the pointed front being covered with diamonds. It was made of satin and lace with tassels falling at the sides.

Another fashionable foreign adaptation was the Arabian tunic, a kind of upper robe arranged after the style of the Greek chiton. It was worn out-of-doors in place of the pelisse. Shawls were worn, too, but severely denounced by some contemporary writers on costume as quite unfit for a British belle. The shawl, however, could be made into a very graceful garment when arranged with taste; and there were beautiful shawls of rich Indian stuff, falling in a pointed train behind, also square Chinese silk shawls with tassels at each corner. When the hot days came, the scarfs with their floating ends were very much in favour.

Veils were worn in different ways. The short white veil which made its appearance in the eighteenth century was succeeded by the large veil thrown carelessly over the hat or bonnet and even the silk cap, and forming quite a drapery about the neck. The long veil hanging from the back of the cap, like a bridal veil, was rather an exceptional fashion, and only worn with full dress. Rich Mechlin lace veils were worn with gipsy hats—a very unsuitable combination. Mechlin lace was quite at variance with the simplicity of the gipsy hat. In 1808 the veil was not very long, only reaching to the throat. It was put on in a loose, untidy way, with the sides hanging out instead of being drawn to the back. Hats and bonnets were all large, and shaded the face more effectually than the tiny sarcenet parasol. The velvet and cloth hats which matched the winter pelisses were very picturesque with their drooping feathers.

There was a great deal of what might be called fancy head-gear worn, both in-doors and for walking. Hats and caps made of silk and satin were seen, of all sorts of indeterminate shapes, trimmed fantastically with tassels and feathers and ribbons. The hair was curled in front very much as it is now, and the open-trimmed hats with ostrich plumes were exceedingly becoming. There were various ways of dressing the hair. Under the turbans and caps nothing could be seen of the hair at the back, but when only bandeaux were worn the hair appears fastened up in a knot rather high, with a few ringlets falling over—a fashion revived many years later. In 1813 the hair was very prettily and simply arranged in a low coil at the back, the front hair in short curls, and a rose coquettishly fastened into the left side, close to the face. Now and then a ringlet would be seen escaping from the large poke or beehive bonnet. Flowers were much worn in the hair and in the caps, which were not removed when the bonnet was put on, the cap-front showing beneath the wide brim. Very high-crowned hats came in about 1814, and a large straw bonnet called the "Oldenburg Poke," after the Duchess of Oldenburg, who visited England in that year with her brother the Czar.

Reverting to evening dress, a fair idea of fashionable ball costume may be gleaned from a gossipy letter in *La Belle Assemblée* for 1807. The writer is describing two dresses prepared for a party for which upwards of six hundred cards were issued. "Mary's is a round dress of white crape, over white satin, with a rich border of the water lily in gold. The body is of white satin, with ornaments of point lace, and edgings of narrow gold trimming. She will wear her hair in irregular curls on the crown of her head, and flowing in ringlets on the left side, so as to play on the shoulder, divided in front of the forehead with a diamond star, representing the passion-flower. My dress is a round gown of white sarcenet, with a French lace put easily full at the feet. A French apron of Paris net, trimmed all round, and at the pockets with wreaths of jessamine; the bosom and sleeves correspondently ornamented. My hair in loose curls, confined with braids on one side and ornamented with a wreath formed of pearl and green foil representing the jessamine. My trinkets are of seed pearls with emerald snaps; and my shoes of white satin with silver rosets." The writer goes on to describe fashionable head-gear and hair ornaments. The hair, we are told, is "variously disposed and ornamented with a handkerchief of lace, bandeaux, stars and demi-wreaths. The diadem and tiara have had their day. A few turbans of plain white or silver muslin, worn on the forehead in the Chinese form, have been lately introduced: they are either ornamented with deep bands of gold or silver or twisted with large white beads. The cap *à la* Mary Queen of Scots is entirely of recent date."

Between 1807 and 1808 there was a faint attempt to lengthen the waist, or, more correctly speaking, to place what passed for the waist-line of the gown a little nearer to the natural waist. But a strong objection prevailed against long waists. They were held in peculiar detestation, regarded as barbarisms, and after the girdle had been lowered an inch or two it went up again. Waists grew shorter than before, and it was not until the century was out of its teens that there was any real effort to put the waist in its proper position.

All through the short-sleeve period gloves were, of course, long. They generally matched the shoes, and we read of lilac and lemon-coloured kid and York tan. With tan gloves, which were very popular, red Morocco slippers were worn. As the dress was usually white, any colour could be used for the adjuncts. The spencer and pelisse almost invariably matched the hat. Foot-gear was as fanciful as in the eighteenth century. Even velvet was considered quite fit for out-door wear in winter. Most of the shoes were low; there was, however, introduced what were called ankle boots, laced up the back; but, as they were made of velvet and kid, they were not much improvement on the slipper.

The war with France having stopped communication between the two countries, we were left, for some time, to our own devices in regard to costume. When at length the Treaty of Peace was signed, in 1814, the English flocked to Paris in great numbers, and very scathing remarks were made by satirical observers on the inelegance of British taste when left unguided by French genius. But the long pelisses and beehive bonnets which came in for condemnation did not deserve the reprobation they incurred, and nothing could have been prettier than the modest, high, muslin robe with the sleeves in small puffs from the shoulder to the wrist, the falling collar and Angoulême straw bonnet showing the hair in small curls in front. "The present fashion," says the *Lady's Magazine* in 1815, "has recalled the privileges of the young; . . . no woman of real taste, unless there be a defect to conceal, would bundle up her arms in a large puckered sleeve or, however beautiful her neck, suffer her robe to fall from her shoulders so as to put her in incessant dread of its dropping off altogether, and thereby to prevent her using her arms with ease or freedom."

The waists in 1814 and 1815 were a trifle

longer, but only for a time; they afterwards rose to their original place. Not only walking-dresses, but dinner and ball dresses were made short, well above the ankle, and trimmed with broad lace round the bottom if the dress were of crapé or muslin. It is satisfactory to find morning dresses becoming more substantial for winter, and merino substituted for muslin in December. Muslin was still worn very late and very early in the year, but silk reps, poplins, and cloths were more used than before.

By 1817 the change which had been creeping into the form of the gown was very noticeable. It was no longer clinging, but stood out from the figure, was always short, and much ornamented. People were clearly tired of the style of the antique which had characterized the costume of the last twenty years, and were beginning to want something less drooping. The waist being still under the arm-pits, it was anything but an improvement to both shorten and widen the skirt, and some of the gowns worn at this period were very shapeless and unbecoming. In evening dresses the bottom of the skirt was made to stand out stiffly as if lined with buckram, and all sorts of fanciful trimmings were introduced—embroidery and scollops in bright colours, gold braid, and fringe.

The bodice had now become so exceedingly

short that it hardly seems worth a mention. In an evening gown with short, puffed sleeves, the bottom of the bodice was in a line with the rim of the sleeve. A figured gauze or silk scarf generally appears hanging over the arm—an inconvenient appendage to an evening costume. As for out-door dress, the carriage dress of the winter of 1818 was as unsuitable as the walking-dress of previous winters. It was more like a *peignoir*, being made of jaconet muslin in the form of a loose robe, a little open at the neck. It was covered with fine embroidery, and the smart French cap of net and blond trimmed with coloured ribbons was a very appropriate finish; but it was a costume for the boudoir, not the park, particularly in dreary November.

In the beginning of 1819, the nation being in mourning for Queen Charlotte, evening dresses were made of black crape over white satin slips, still with the very short bodice and sleeve. Black cloth pelisses, lined with white sarcenet and trimmed with white silk cord, were worn for walking; bonnets were of black Leghorn, trimmed with blond and satin. Black bombazine dresses were worn, though it was January; but to people who had been used to wearing white muslin in mid-winter, the incongruity was not apparent. The next month every one was in colours again, in white jaconet muslins,

Leghorn bonnets trimmed with white satin, and fine cloth pelisses. For evening, coloured French crapes were worn, with ruchings of satin round the skirt which was short, like the walking-dress. Satin shoes with sandals were in fashion then.

The revival of what we call the Empire style makes the fashions of this period tolerably familiar to every one. But revived fashions are always modified by the taste of the age in which they reappear. We recall a fashion to give variety to dress, not because the particular mode restored is in itself specially commendable, and the object is attained if the salient points of the costume indicate the bygone period. Consequently, we get a curious confounding of styles. The desire of 1892–3 to wear "Empire" gowns, and yet preserve the waist and the outline of the figure, has resulted in the evolution of a gown that will puzzle the future chroniclers of costume. During the first twenty years of the century there were no waists; gowns were girdled under the arms, but the line thus formed could not be called a waist.

The period following the fall of the Empire was a very unsettled period for costume in France. The occupation of Paris by the Allied Armies, after the battle of Waterloo, gave a cosmopolitan character to French costume. Even in the midst of the national humiliation fashion asserted its influence, and turned to account the presence of the invaders, borrowing a hint, now from one and now from another. Among an imitative people like the French, the most trifling events have always been seized upon. Even the arrival of a giraffe in 1827—the first ever seen in France—did not escape the fashion-mongers, who devised gowns and coiffures *à la giraffe*, a style which did not last long, but a survival of which was to be seen in the high tortoiseshell combs worn in 1830. In like manner the foreign expeditions and invasions of Napoleon had brought in all sorts of bizarre fashions; and skilful milliners, adapting themselves to the whim of the day, invented a great variety of fancy costumes. "*La mode* at Paris," writes Mrs. Jameson in her *Lady's Diary*, 1826, " is a spell of wondrous power; it is most like what we should call in England a rage, a mania, a torrent sweeping down the bounds between good and evil, sense and nonsense, upon whose surface straws and egg-shells float into notoriety, while the gold and the marble are buried and hidden till its force be spent. The rage for cashmeres and little dogs has lately given way to a rage for *Le Solitaire*, a romance written, I believe, by a certain Vicomte d'Arlincourt. *Le Solitaire* rules the imagination the taste, the dress, and half Paris. . . . Men dress their hair and throw their cloaks about them *à la Solitaire*: bonnets and caps, flounces and ribbons, are all *à la Solitaire*."

Towards the twenties there was a revulsion from the style of the antique, both in France and England. Its simplicity was felt to be monotonous. Ornamentation cloys, but not so soon, for it admits of so much variety. The plain muslin gowns, which had been thought the perfection of good dressing, were discarded. The skirts were shortened, and trimmed with flounces, puffings, and ruchings. Sleeves were made a little full, and a single-puff on the shoulder did duty for the sleeve of a ball gown. The leg-of-mutton sleeve appeared in France as early as 1820, but went out again to reappear towards the thirties. Everything became smarter and more piquant.

There was a decided difference in the position of the waist; it was getting down to its real place in 1820. Short, daintily trimmed skirts, with the waist in its natural position, sleeves short and slightly puffed, the neck of the gown cut low and rounded over the shoulders, made a very becoming style, much prettier than was seen subsequently. There was little exaggeration in any part of the costume, except a tendency to over-trim. In 1823 carriage dresses became much more sensible.

Instead of ladies shivering in winter in muslin gowns, they were wrapped in rich, comfortable taffety pelisses bordered with fur, fur tippets, and big muffs. All the muffs were very large at this time. Matrons took to wearing the pelisse as an in-door costume, when it was called the pelisse robe. It was almost exactly like the out-door pelisse, except that it generally opened in front over a petticoat. These home dresses more and more resembled the walking-costume, all the pelisses being tightly fitting as they were worn in Paris.

The style of coiffure changed too, but not for the better. The hair was twisted up high into a little crown at the back, in a stiff, strained fashion. The younger ladies wore flowers and combs more than turbans and caps for evening dress, or else white satin and tulle hats. The hats worn at the opera were very elaborate, with many feathers. In 1825 the hair was arranged in high poufs drawn to the left side, with a few drooping ringlets, and the short curls still in front. Curls were universal, and there were all sorts of fanciful ways of arranging them.

Sleeves had not yet attained their maximum width, but in 1827 they were worn *en gigot*, stiffened at the shoulder, so that the outer garment, the shawl, pelisse, or cloak, should not crush them

Pelerines covering the shoulders, with long ends in front, and fastening at the neck and waist, were worn with morning dresses. They were made just to meet the top of the puffed sleeve, where they extended in a point, which gave great width to the shoulders. The sleeve continued to grow; the puffing extended further down the arm, and with some of the evening gowns there were long, wide gauze or crape sleeves over the short satin or silk sleeve of the gown. The white tulle dresses, over satin slips, frequently had tulle sleeves puffed all the way down from shoulder to wrist.

In 1828 the flounces to the walking-dresses were very deep; two flounces covered half the skirt. In conformity with the swelling sleeve and stiffer, wider skirts, the hats became larger, and were more heavily trimmed. Dress hats were quite portentous with frilled lace and blond, flowers, ribbons, and lappets. The coiffure reached the climax of unbecomingness. The short front curls were disposed on each side of the parting, and the rest of the hair was fastened up in ugly loops with which ribbon loops were interwoven, the whole mass standing up erect from the crown of the head. Large plumes of the Bird of Paradise, and tufts of marabou feathers were fastened into these loops for dressy occasions.

At the close of 1828 it was announced that cloth dresses would be fashionable for the winter, and a writer in the *Lady's Magazine* solemnly warns her readers against the danger of wearing such dresses in-doors. People were still so accustomed to light materials all the year round, that cloth dresses seemed unreasonably warm. "They are very comfortable as a high dress," says the correspondent, "in morning walks, requiring only a pelerine in addition; but there is much to be said against them: never ought they to be retained as a fireside costume; for perhaps the next evening is devoted to a dress party or a ball, when the thinness of the texture and the nakedness of the neck and arms are sure to be the causes of violent colds, often ending in pulmonary complaints." Violent colds were more likely to be caught by wearing muslin dresses in the street than cloth dresses at the fireside. What would such a writer think of the present generation, cowering over fires in the thickest of tweeds and serges? Happily, in our revivals of fashions, we have not revived the custom of ignoring the seasons in the choice of materials.

The growing plainness which was observable in men's dress at the close of the eighteenth century continued to be characteristic of the costume of the nineteenth century. Wraxall, writing in 1815, laments the change which had taken place during the last forty years. "That costume," he says, "which is now confined to the Levée or the Drawing-room, was then worn by persons of condition with few exceptions, everywhere and every day." The simplicity, or, as some called it, the slovenliness, affected by Charles James Fox and his friends in the House of Commons passed on to the clubs, and from the clubs the "contagion" spread through all fashionable London. In 1808, gentlemen are described as acting like a foil to the ladies, and the plainness of their attire is commended as enabling them to be ready at a moment's notice for anything that might arise. The "trousered beau," should he be even suddenly required to accompany some of the fair sex on an aquatic excursion, would not be embarrassed by considerations of costume. Certainly a gentleman in silk stockings, velvet knee-breeches, powdered wig, cocked hat, and sword might feel encumbered if called upon to handle a pair of sculls.

The cocked hat was only worn for full dress, except by some of the older generation, who liked to retain the fashions of their youth. For morning dress the high-crowned silk beaver hat, with brim rather large and curling, was the general wear.

Nobody, except for Court dress, wore wigs or powder, save only members of the learned professions, who kept up the elaborate hair-dressing of the previous period. During the first decade of the century, some of the older generation still powdered their hair. In *Pride and Prejudice*, Mr. Bennet, whose family were certainly not behind the times in fashion, speaks of his powdering-gown. He threatens, when misfortune next befalls him, to sit in his library in nightcap and powdering-gown.* Pantaloons took the place of knee-breeches; they were made of plain, light-coloured cloth, and fitted very tightly. When striped cloth was first introduced it was regarded as very plebeian, and only fit for wearing in muddy weather, or at the seaside. Hessian boots were a good deal worn; but they did not altogether banish shoes from morning costume.

All sorts of colours were used for coats and waistcoats—olive, brown, green, and buff. For evening dress, however, blue coats with gilt buttons, and white waistcoats of Marseilles quilting were generally worn. But in 1835, black coats were also worn, and coloured waistcoats. At very fashionable assemblies gentlemen were seen in embroidered Court suits. Colonel Newcome, when

* Jane Austen, *Pride and Prejudice*.

he went to his first evening party the day after his return from India, was arrayed in the costume of the twenties—viz. a blue swallow-tailed coat with yellow buttons, and very high velvet collar, "a high waist indicated by two lapelles and a pair of buttons high up in the wearer's back, a white waistcoat and scarlet under-waistcoat, and a pair of the never-failing duck trousers."* Knee-breeches, silk stockings, and shoes completed the evening costume. Trousers were not altogether inadmissible, but were looked upon as not quite correct. The ladies' committee of Almack's decreed that no gentleman should attend the balls given by the club at Willis's Rooms in trousers. One evening the Duke of Wellington presented himself so attired. His entrance was barred by an official, who courteously observed, "Your Grace cannot be admitted in trousers." The Duke made no remonstrance, but walked away. This was in 1814.

Morning and evening coats were for some years identical in shape. In 1820 the morning coats were still short and square in front, but by 1824 the younger men had taken to wearing something which approached the shape of a modern frock coat. Coat tails were growing shorter. Overcoats, which in

* *The Newcomes.*

winter had large fur collars, fitted tightly at the waist, and were rather full in the skirt. Stays were evidently worn by the beaux, and false calves under the elastic stockinet pantaloons, which were fashionable at one time. After the tight pantaloons came Cossack trousers. By 1830-32 trousers had assumed their present shape. They were neither tight nor baggy. Straps were generally worn, and, when trousers became part of full dress, silk straps were used. Collars were high, and both muslin and silk cravats were worn. There was an attempt to introduce black cravats into evening dress, but it was not successful, and the fashion disappeared very quickly. The coat sleeves were long, not like the modern coat sleeve, but fitting tightly at the wrist, with the cuff projecting over the hand. In 1832 it became fashionable to wear a large cloak instead of a great-coat. There were also cloaks specially adapted for wearing with full dress, made of coloured cloth and lined with silk. The Polish cloak was a novelty of that period; it was made with a cape to button across the front, and could be worn either single or double.

"The fashions of this country," says Goede, who visited England early in the nineteenth century, "are simple and harmonious; the shape perhaps does not always please the eye, but the colour is invariably becoming, and the *tout ensemble* agreeable. Nothing would appear more ridiculous than to see a man half-fashionably clad; as the coat is cut so must the waistcoat and breeches correspond; nor would this suffice, unless the shape of the hat and exact measure of the boot were in perfect unison: every reform therefore must be radical."

CHAPTER II.

1830–1850.

Big sleeves—Pelerines—Hair-dressing and head-gear—Colours—Out-door costume—Male costume—The chimney-pot hat.

> "What will not length of time be able to change?"
> CLAUDIANUS.

THE fashions of the thirties, which we have lately been reviving, were simply huge exaggerations of the modes of the twenties. The slightly full sleeve and the simple round skirt were developed into the huge excrescence called a sleeve, which hung like a bag from the shoulder, and a distended petticoat which looked as if courting the crinoline. A few years previously costume had a bewitching air of innocence; it was the dress of the *ingénue*. But by 1830 it had become thoroughly distorted.

The first thing was to spoil the shoulders. The low-necked gowns, instead of being rounded at the top, were cut straight, giving an ugly, angular look to the shoulders, and an impression that the dress was on the point of slipping off. But the sleeve was the great feature of costume. It was so big that it swallowed up the bodice. Between the shoulder and the elbow it swelled out into a monstrous balloon. From the elbow to the wrist it was tight. Silk dresses had the sleeves wadded at the top. Some sleeves had large ribbon bows with broad ends streaming from the shoulders, a hideous and meaningless fashion.

The skirts being very short, displaying the ankle fully, made the sleeves look the more exaggerated, and it was, perhaps, with the idea of redressing the balance that the skirts were made fuller. Between the skirt and the sleeve, the waist, enclosed in a plain band about two inches wide, looked very small, and the figure very narrow. There was no fulness whatever in the bodice itself, not a pleat or a gather; it was fitted as tightly as possible. But from the shoulders, forming a top to the sleeve, which needed no addition, came the *revers*, shaped like a cape at the back and coming down to a point in front. Sometimes folds of stuff were laid across the bodice at the top; this crossed drapery, which is so familiar a style of trimming, being much in favour about 1832. A straight, short cape, only a few inches deep, forming a hard line round the neck, was fastened on as a finish to evening gowns, and it is difficult to conceive of anything more unbecoming. Low dresses were always spoiled by the straightness on the shoulders.

The cape and the *revers* were varieties of the pelerine. All drapery was *à la pelerine*. The outdoor pelerine with the turn-down collar made a pretty mantle for walking. There were pelerines of all sizes and various shapes, pelerines which ended at the waist and just draped the shoulders, and pelerines which covered the bodice and had long, broad ends hanging in front or crossed at the back.

Gowns were all short for evening as well as morning, and there was no skimping of sleeves in the evening gowns. They were short but very full, and large blond sleeves down to the wrist were often worn over the sleeves of the dress. Blond lace was much used for trimming. The skirts being so wide, it is not surprising to find seven and eight breadths of silk required, and to make them stand out well they were lined with stiff muslin. A variety in the shape of evening gowns was created by the tunic-robe. This was a sleeveless bodice with pointed shoulder-pieces and the skirt opening in front, showing the under-dress, which was made about two inches longer and of a contrasting colour. The tunic was fitted tightly with a waist-belt, in the

usual way. A great many ball dresses were made of tulle over satin and sarcenet, the upper robe being caught up at the sides with knots of ribbons and bunches of flowers. Coloured gauzes, plain and figured, and crapes embroidered in chenille were also used. Dinner dresses were made with half-high *corsages*.

For walking and house dresses cashmere and embroidered cambric were worn. We do not hear now of the riding-habit being used as a promenade costume. It seemed confined to its legitimate purpose. The summer habit of 1832 was a dark cloth skirt, long and exceedingly full; a cambric canezou—the counterpart of the modern blouse— with sleeves full to the elbow and tight to the wrist; a high-crowned straw hat, worn a little on one side; and a long gauze veil. A frilled white petticoat was usually worn under the skirt. Riding-trousers had not then been invented.

At no period was the back view of a lady's costume so unpleasing. The dressmaker's art is shown in the cut of the back; any one can make the front presentable. But the dressmakers of the thirties were at a great disadvantage. Not the most skilful of hands could have made the backs of the gowns anything but ugly, particularly in the case of evening gowns. The low, straight neck unrelieved by frill of muslin or lace, the stiff, round waist, and the enormous sleeves made a *tout ensemble* the effect of which was rendered worse by the style of hair-dressing, which was not only unbecoming in itself, but unsuited to the mode of dress.

Very little alteration was made in the coiffure. The loops were still worn, the back hair all gathered up tightly from the nape of the neck. The front hair was parted in the centre, with bunches of stiff curls on each side; or sometimes combed flatly down or in close plaits. With full dress the thin circlet of gold or pearls was worn across the forehead, or a small wreath mounted on black velvet. Terrible-looking ornamental pins, significantly termed poignards and stilettos, were also worn. Later on, the hair was dressed quite flat on the top of the head, and the front turned back over the ears in loops. The back was done up very stiffly in small braids, not close to the head, but standing out in bows. Some fashion-magazines describe this knot at the back as *à la Grecque;* but nothing so strained and ungraceful ever disfigured the head of a Greek girl. Plumes of feathers were fastened into the hair in all sorts of indescribable ways, at grotesque angles. Regular head-dresses of gauze and feathers were worn at fashionable parties, as well as the large satin hats and black velvet *bérets*—wide-brimmed low-crowned hats, turned up on the left side. What were called half-caps were worn in the early forties; they were circular head-dresses set well back from the front, and trimmed with bunches of ribbons and flowers at each side, over the ears. Hats and bonnets were a little smaller then.

In 1835 we read that, at a very smart party given in London, only two or three of the elder ladies wore hats or head-dresses. "At the back of the head were edifices of hair of various kinds, and in these the feathers were fastened. Five or six of the youngest of the ladies had nothing on the head; the others, old and young, wore a number of white ostrich feathers. . . . Here and there, as an exception, was seen a blue, red, or yellow feather; in front was a diadem, a flower, or an ornament of the most sparkling brilliants." Bonnets do not seem to have been worn by fashionable brides, but long veils, fastened to the hair at the back, and falling nearly to the bottom of the skirt. Except the veil there was nothing to distinguish a bridal costume from any ordinary white evening dress. Wedding-gowns were made with low necks, like ball gowns.

Orange blossoms, "those touching emblems of female purity imported by us from France, where people's daughters are universally sold in marriage," were not in vogue even as late as 1848, when *Vanity Fair* was published.

The long cloak for driving, the pelisse, or redingote, and the pelerine for walking formed the usual out-door garb. Some very gay opera cloaks were in vogue; they were all long, like the carriage cloaks. Fur tippets and muffs continued in fashion, and the long fur boa came in for evening wear in place of the silk scarf. Evening dresses were occasionally trimmed with fur.

Colours continued to be very pronounced, and were combined with an audacity which has, happily, seldom been equalled since. For instance, a promenade costume for the early part of 1836 consisted of a "Swedish blue satin robe, black-violet mantelet, lined with blue satin and trimmed with black lace. The mantelet is of a large size, made quite up to the throat, and cut so as to display the bust in a very advantageous manner. Hat of bright emerald green velvet, a moderate-sized brim, and perpendicular crown. The brim is trimmed with blond and roses; the crown with ribbons to correspond, and two ostrich feathers." Wives of city traders living over their husbands' shops could not pretend to the fashions of the West End, but they were still more astonishing in their choice and arrangement of colours. Mrs. Bungay, wife of the celebrated

Mr. Bungay of Paternoster Row, with whom Pendennis and his friends had many dealings, went out to pay her bills in "a gorgeous shot-silk dress, which flamed with red and purple; she wore a yellow shawl and had red flowers inside her bonnet, and a brilliant light-blue parasol."* The pelerines were growing very large: they were quite mantles, and gave a matronly air to the wearer. The scarf was still in fashion for summer. Some walking-dresses were made with the bodice turned back over a cambric chemisette—the equivalent of our shirt—only with the addition of a lace ruff round the throat; and no mantle was worn with these costumes.

Between 1836 and 1837 the style of the gown was slightly changed. Instead of the round waistband the bodice was pointed, and the sleeves were a little smaller. They were put in very low, so that the shoulder was quite flat, and the puff fell over the elbow in a point. Evening gowns had the sleeves made with several small puffs and gaugings. The shape of the bodice was the same at the top, cut very low and straight on the shoulders. The bodices of morning gowns were all made with pelerine-shaped drapery. How greatly the sleeve had diminished may be seen from the way in which

* *Pendennis.*

the out-door pelerine was worn, wrapped round the shoulders and drawn tightly over the arms, which would have been impossible when the very big leg of-mutton sleeves were worn. The ends of the pelerine were sometimes crossed at the back; they were always very broad, and edged with lace or fur. Sleeves of evening gowns were not very short; the lace frill brought them to the elbow, but the neck was cut quite low, like present Court dress.

Skirts were longer; ankles ceased to be visible and only the point of the narrow-toed shoe peeps from beneath the spreading petticoat, which was propped out with stiff muslin. Deep flounces, narrow flounces, and ribbon bows all down the front adorned the skirts, which were put in very full all round. The bodice was frequently laced down the back, or fastened with hooks and eyes, to the intense discomfort of the wearer, who, in either case could not perform her toilet unaided. This was the age of the large brooches which were used to fasten the collar or the pelerine, worn with the half-high morning gown. Some of these brooches survive still as heirlooms, and a use may yet be found for them.

Spencers reappeared with the neck cut low. The Paris correspondent to the *Court Magazine* writing in 1839, says: "Spencers are decidedly

adopted by the nobility. . . . They are only half-high. How will the English ladies like exposing their fair necks to the scorching rays of the sun?" Every succeeding year dress became more patchy and ungraceful. Meaningless bows were dotted about the gowns and the voluminous mantles; large silk aprons, much trimmed, were worn indoors, and the skirts of the gowns began to be made in two pieces, an under-skirt, and an upper-skirt opening down the front, edged with lace or *bouillons* of stuff.

The accessories to costume were all small: muffs had shrunk considerably; bouquets were mere nosegays; fans looked intended for ornament rather than use, and the same might be said of the parasols, which were hardly large enough to cover the bonnets. Colours remained very bright. "Lady Crawley," writes Becky Sharp to Amelia, "is made to put on the brightest pea-green in her wardrobe" to do honour to the great rich Miss Crawley when that lady chose to pay a visit to the country.*

In the early autumn of 1840 a fashionable walking-costume was a redingote of Scotch plaid, made of *mousseline de laine*, "the colours as brilliant as possible." It was a season when plaids and

* *Vanity Fair.*

mixtures were much more used than plain colours, and shot silks were in favour. In the same year the novelty of nankeen dresses was introduced, which necessitated a very tight corset. These nankeen dresses were made quite high to the throat, unlike most of the morning gowns. They appeared first in Paris, where they excited some dismay, and were regarded as startling innovations, apparently on account of their close, severe style. "The ladies will be taking care of their shapes again, as our grandmothers did in days of yore. A stoop and one of those tight corsages will never do together, that so a lady who cannot mend her carriage must e'en content herself with wearing a full corsage and being *out of the fashion.*"

In 1840 Paris was getting tired of flounces, and the newest fashions transmitted to England were tucked skirts, and skirts without any trimming. They were exceedingly wide, and the bodices rather long and pointed. To have a small waist was one of the first articles of faith in the fashionable world, and to accomplish this without discomfort the following advice was given by one of the authorities: "Have your dress made with a long waist; have your petticoats gathered into very broad bands, cut on the crossway, and with a point in front, so as not to have gathers under the point of your dress; let the petticoat be made of *crinoline*, or wear what we call a *jupon à tournure*, which is a petticoat made of a very thick and stiff cotton or thread material, not dimity, but a sort of honeycomb pattern all over; this will make your dress appear sufficiently full (*bouffante*) and form a proper contrast to the waist, thereby sparing the necessity and agony as well as injury of tight-lacing." The advice was timely, for in the following year we read that "tight corsages still take precedence of all others, and this in every costume from the morning *negligé* to the *robe de bal.*" Sleeves were variable, made with small *gigots* at the top, with *bouillons* all the way down, and also perfectly plain and close. The full sleeve never went quite out, but was always cropping up in some shape or other.

In 1842 stomachers and trains returned, though trains were not worn at balls. But in Paris they were worn in the streets, for a wag wrote in one of the papers: "The administration of 'la ville de Paris' has it in contemplation to do away with the scavengers in our good city, as they say that it is a useless expense to pay men for doing that which the ladies so kindly perform gratis in walking through our fashionable promenades."

In 1843 the skirts worn in England were still

long enough to be inconvenient, but the front was a little shortened; and did not quite touch the ground. There was not much change in out-door costume. Mantles for summer were of the pelerine shape, drawn in to the waist at the back, and large enough to cover the bodice completely. Bonnets, in spite of an intimation that they were to become smaller, still looked out of all proportion to the tiny fringed parasols. There was a very matronly air about costume; it suggested a quiet dignified mien, and required a sedate carriage. The arms were folded firmly to keep the mantle in its place, and a delicate lace pocket-handkerchief fluttered in one hand.

In 1844 flounces were very deep, but not at all full. Many dresses were made with double skirts, in tunic form, and in two colours. Gimp and fringe trimmings were used on morning gowns, and the sleeves were tight and plain with a frill of lace at the wrist. The neck of the bodice was sometimes high, sometimes half-high. Evening bodices were still cut very straight on the shoulders, and finished with a lace bertha or a canezou of Indian muslin, embroidered and pleated. The canezou was shaped something like the pelerine. There were various styles of coiffure for full dress: sometimes caps were worn with lace lappets, which made a pretty shade to the face; and a wreath of flowers encircling the head formed an appropriate accompaniment to a ball costume. Ringlets were much worn in 1845, and for years after. The day-caps had ribbon ends as long as bonnet strings, and, being tied under the chin, gave the young women a very elderly appearance. All the caps seemed to be adapted to women of advanced years whose hair was scanty, as the back of the head was completely covered.

Gloves varied from long to short with the sleeves. Gloves reaching to the elbow were worn with the short-sleeved evening gowns; and there were gloves of four-button length, edged with lace and ruchings, and gloves with only one or two buttons. Some gloves were laced up the arm, which secured a very good fit. Lace mittens were worn all through the thirties and forties, being more fashionable at some seasons than others. They were used both in-doors and out-of-doors, but were considered rather half-dress in-doors, and worn with afternoon costumes.

There is little to be said about juvenile costume, for, as formerly, it was mainly a copy of the dress of grown-up people. There were no artists to design charming frocks for little girls in those days. They strutted about in frilled cambric trousers and short wide petticoats—quaint little figures, with only the natural grace of childhood to render them pleasing.

As for the "young gentleman" of the period, he was a facsimile of his elders. Only very young boys wore the short coat, the forerunner of the Eton jacket. Master George Osborne, "though scarcely eleven years of age, wore straps and the most beautiful little boots, like a man. He had gilt spurs, and a gold-headed whip, and a fine pin in his handkerchief; and the neatest little kid gloves which Lamb's Conduit Street could furnish." He had "little white waistcoats for evening parties, and little cut-velvet waistcoats for dinners, and a dear little darling shawl dressing-gown—for all the world like a little man."*

There was not much change in men's dress for some years. The dark colours for morning dress introduced by George IV., who was famous for his dark-blue frock coat with fur collar, continued to be used. The morning costume of a dandy is described by Thackeray as consisting of a green coat with big steel buttons, a red-striped waistcoat, neckcloths high and voluminous, buskins, and very shiny Hessian boots. The military frogged coat was very fashionable, and a great deal of braiding and velvet was used as trimming.

* *Vanity Fair.*

Coloured coats and trousers for evening dress were worn into the forties. The coats had velvet collars, and the skirts were faced with silk. They were not quite so swallow-tailed then. A great deal of attention was given to waistcoats, which, for full dress, were of white or coloured satin and velvet, handsomely embroidered. Joseph Sedley, when he was going to town, selected "a crimson satin, embroidered with gold butterflies, and a black and red velvet tartan with white stripes, and a rolling collar, with which, and a rich blue satin stock and a gold pin, consisting of a five-barred gate with a horseman in pink enamel jumping over it — he thought he might make his entry into London with some dignity."* Pendennis, when he went home from the university for the long vacation, astonished his mother and Laura with his gorgeous velvet waistcoats and his embroidered cravats.† Waistcoats were very short, but not cut so low as they are now, except for Court costume.

The tall silk hat, introduced from France about 1840, superseded the beaver hat, which had been generally worn before. There had been silk hats with "felt bodies" made previously in England, but the French silk hat was thought a great improvement, and was at once adopted. The English

* *Vanity Fair.* † *Pendennis.*

beaver-hat makers soon learned to rival the French in the making of silk hats. The chimney-pot hat is the most remarkable example of the persistence of a fashion which every one joins in abusing. Of course it has undergone some variations, but they are slight. There was the Wellington hat with the yeoman crown, the Anglesea hat with the bell-shaped crown, the D'Orsay hat with ribbed silk binding and a large bow to the band. The eccentric Earl of Harrington, who considerately wore a sage-green hat when he walked in his garden, in order not to frighten the birds, gave his name to a top-hat with an odd-looking square brim. This same Earl tested his hats by standing on them. He wore beaver hats weighing a little over twenty ounces, and for which he was accustomed to pay three guineas. The Prince Consort, who effected a great improvement in military hats, did not attempt to relieve civilians from the discomfort of their unsightly head-gear, though, for his own part, he showed a preference for light felt hats in summer. No leader of male fashions has ever seriously tried to interfere with the top-hat. Such as it was half a century ago it is to-day, and will not be displaced by anything short of a complete revolution in men's costume.

CHAPTER III.

1850–1870.

Shapeless style of costume—The crinoline—Substitutes for the crinoline—General fashions—Jewellery—Trimmings—Tight lacing—Fall of the crinoline.

"There are flagrant follies in fashion which must be endured while they reign, and never appear ridiculous till they are out of fashion."—*Curiosities of Literature.*

WITH the fifties we approach a period that, as far as fashion is concerned, one would wish to see erased from history. Dress that is hugely extravagant or grotesque possesses an interest from its strangeness; but dress that is merely ugly has nothing to recommend it to notice. The end of the forties and the whole of the fifties are more open to the charge of downright ugliness than any period in the nineteenth century. When the crinoline came, to the ugly was superadded the ridiculous. We who laugh at the whimsicalities of the eighteenth century ought to sit in dust and ashes for the barbarisms of our own age. Forty years ago both Paris and London had absolutely lost the art of dressing. Costume was shapeless; colours were crude and horribly mixed; and there was too much of almost everything. There were too many flowers, too many ornaments, too many ribbons, and, above all, too many petticoats and too much skirt. In reviving the Empire and 1830 fashions a good deal of modification has had to be introduced to make them acceptable; but a revival of the fashions of the fifties would indeed require a master hand. It is not only that we have to dread being made grotesque by the crinoline—that would be bad enough; but the crinoline is, after all, only a part, though a very large part, of the disfigurements of that period. The crinoline would carry with it flounces, double skirts, basques, bows, and balloon-like mantles. It would be impossible to imitate the fashions of the fifties and sixties with any approach to correctness, and preserve the semblance of good taste.

There is, fortunately, one characteristic of that period which will always militate against its revival. It had the fatal quality of making all the young women appear middle-aged. There was no youthfulness in those days; the very children looked strangely grown-up. It is difficult to believe that girls danced, flirted, and frolicked as they do now, and that those women whom we see with their hair drawn down flatly over their ears were really young wives in their twenties.

The first thing that strikes one in comparing the 1830 fashions with the fashions of the forties and early fifties is the difference in the sleeves. The shape was reversed. Instead of sleeves *en gigot* we had sleeves *en pagode*—that is, narrow at the shoulder and wide at the bottom. Of course this brought in the under-sleeve, not an ungraceful, but an extremely inconvenient fashion, which kept its place with great persistency. Those whose memories will carry them back twenty or five and twenty years will remember how sleeves *en pagode* were still in vogue, especially among young girls, and how dressing for a party involved fastening on with elastic or tape those uncomfortable under-sleeves, which were always slipping down and dangling into cups of tea and custards. Sometimes they were gathered into a band at the wrist, when they were certainly less in the way, but had very much the appearance of night-gown sleeves. These were shaped like the bishop sleeves, which were afterwards worn so commonly.

Crinolines did not make their appearance until 1854, but for several years previously skirts had been so wide and ungainly that the crinolines, when they came at last, seemed only a natural evolution. It was not enough that skirts should have huge, flopping flounces; they were made with a double skirt above the flounces. There were vandyked and scolloped flounces, flounces edged with lace and fringe, flounces plain and flounces headed with gimp or velvet. Ball dresses were generally of crape or tarlatan, and were profusely trimmed with lace. The sleeves were made quite short, and gloves were worn short too. In 1850 brocades and damasks were much in fashion, and worn by quite young ladies for dinner dresses. Moire antique was also worn, and continued to be popular for evening gowns for many years.

Silk was more used for day wear than at present, there not being such a large choice of woollen materials. Every lady felt that a silk dress was necessary to her self-respect. She went to church on Sunday, she paid calls, she sat at home in the afternoons in a silk dress. People in those days had best clothes. Among the middle classes silk attire denoted a certain standard of gentility to which all desired to attain. It was one of the marks of a "lady"—a term used then to denote a woman who was not obliged to earn her living, or do any kind of useful work. The fashionable world, of course, dressed several times a day, as now, but middle-class people, who still dined in the middle of the day, and entertained each other at tea and supper parties, had their best and everyday gowns, mantles, and bonnets. Mantles were large, to suit the wide skirts, and were trimmed with fringe, lace, jet, gimp, beads, ruchings—every variety of ornament that could be applied. In summer they were made of silk, and in winter of velvet and cloth.

It was a great period, too, for shawls—coloured shawls with plenty of pattern, shawls with light grounds and gay flowers, for Paisley shawls, which were made in imitation of the Indian shawls; and, for those few who could afford them, there were the real Cashmere shawls. The buxom widow, Mrs. Mackenzie, when she went to call on Mr. Pendennis wore a handsome India shawl over a rich silk dress, and carried "a neat parasol of blue, with pale yellow lining." Her bonnet was trimmed "with a profusion of poppies, bluebells, and ears of corn." Sometimes the shawl was folded so as to appear round, but more often worn with the point at the back.

Bonnets were round and open in front, not fitting close to the head. Caps ceased to be worn under the bonnets, and, to fill up the space, a quilling of lace was put inside the rim, and flowers were fastened under the front. The bonnet was large at the back, covering the hair completely, and had a curtain of lace. In summer, tulle bonnets were worn, and fancy straws of all sorts; in winter, velvet and beaver, all very much trimmed with ribbons, feathers, and lace. They varied in size from season to season, and the shape gradually changed from very open fronts to fronts fitting close to the head. White bonnets were very popular, and those who wished to keep their summer bonnets fresh for the next season were advised to put them in a band-box, first pasting the lid with paper, and to lay a wax candle inside. When the bonnet was again required, it would be found to have preserved its colour, while the candle had acquired a saffron hue. Bonnets appear to have had a tendency to fly off the head, substantial as they looked, and had to be pinned on as they are now. An ingenious Frenchman invented a spring for keeping the bonnet in its place. When will some mechanical genius arise and deliver this generation from the treacherous skewers?

In the sixties, bonnets became high and pointed in front, rising up in a peak. But there was no improvement from year to year; they were consistently ugly throughout. It was in 1865 that the objectionable fashion was introduced of wearing insects as millinery, a fashion which was very slow in going out. " Little insects of all kinds, especially flies, are good wear in bonnets," says a fashion-journal. The "little insects" were fixed on to flowers to make them look natural. Ladybirds would be seen perched on to a bunch of white violets, for instance. The hats were hardly more becoming than the bonnets. They had rather high crowns, and the brims were turned up slightly all round. Veils were tied on with a string, and the hair was fastened up in a shapeless lump, enclosed in a net. Even little girls of eight years old wore their hair in nets—not invisible nets, but very obvious silk nets, spangled with jet. Loops and plaits also continued to be worn. The front hair was parted in the centre, and combed down plainly on each side, as before, making a loop over the ears, while the alternative to this style was to have bunches of ringlets.

In 1865 the long Alexandra curl was the prevailing fashion, and the only graceful fashion in hair-dressing that misguided period ever adopted. For evening dress every one wore flowers in abundance on the hair. Girls used no other decoration, and the older ladies had elaborate lace head-dresses, mounted on wire and gauze, into which they contrived to introduce a perfect garden.

Feathers were rarely seen except with Court costume. The artificial flower trade flourished exceedingly in Paris, whence our supplies came.

In 1853 there was a rumour from Paris that the paniers or hoop-petticoats of former days were to be revived. At that time flounces were lined with stiff muslin, sometimes with whalebone, and rolls of stiffening propped out the bottom of the dress. What were called crinoline petticoats were very much worn. The material known as crinoline was a stiff, unpliable stuff, adapted for making a dress stand out well from the figure. But our grandmothers still shrank from the idea of hoops, though they had come to the verge of the fashion they professed to dread. When people heard of paniers or hoops coming in, they said they hoped it was only a false alarm. There was something like a crinoline scare in England in 1853, just as there has been forty years later. The worst predictions were fulfilled. In 1854 "la crinoline parut! Elle ressuscita l'époque des paniers. Elle fut disgracieuse," says M. Challamel.

The appearance of the crinoline violently agitated the Parisian dames; indeed, every Frenchwoman felt that a crisis had arrived. The question was not debated long. The example of the Empress Eugénie was all-powerful, and the crinoline took its place as *the* mode of the year, and not only of that year, but of many a year to follow. It did not edge its way in modestly and tentatively, in small, insinuating shape, but came full-grown. "The hoops of our grandmothers cannot have been much, if at all wider than the skirts of a fashionable lady of the present day," wrote one of the fashion-journals in 1854. There were two kinds of crinolines—the skeleton, consisting of hoops of steel, and crinolines which were complete petticoats. Those who did not take readily to the new invention puffed out their dresses with all sorts of stiff petticoats, made of coarse calico and other materials. The weight dragging from the waist must have been very injurious and uncomfortable. It was found that the crinoline did not adapt itself to ball dresses; it was too hard and unyielding to wear under diaphanous tarlatan robes. So a number of petticoats made with flounces were substituted. In 1856 we read that "many belles now wear fourteen in evening dress. They go to a ball standing up in their carriages, and stand between the dances for fear of crushing their dress and fourteen petticoats." It was a busy time again for laundresses. Prodigious quantities of starch were consumed, for petticoats were no use unless freshly got up.

There was a great deal of muslin, cambric, and other white washing material used in the fifties and sixties. Cambric trousers were worn by little girls and very little boys, trimmed elaborately with frills and embroidery. There were chemisettes and lace sleeves, the white *piqué* dresses, which stood out like a board, and muslin dresses of all sorts. By-and-by a clamour was raised against the multiplicity of petticoats; they were so troublesome and expensive that a slight reduction was made in their number.

As for the crinoline, it was no use trying to dethrone it until some thorough reform was made in the whole style of dress. In 1857 there was so much fulness put into the skirts, that it was found impossible to make them "sit well" without a crinoline. A correct crinoline at that time consisted of "four narrow steels each covered with tape, and run into a calico slip; the steel nearest the waist should be four nails from it, and should be one and three quarter yards in length. The remaining three should be only two and a half yards, and placed, one at six nails' distance from the upper steel, the other two each at two nails' distance from the second steel. None must meet in front by a quarter of a yard except the one nearest the waist. These petticoats are most comfortable, never injure or bend, are easily folded in getting into a carriage, and, more than all, the dress sits most gracefully over them." It is impossible to credit the last assertion. No dress at that period could sit gracefully; it was so radically defective; its form was so ungainly. One is sorry to hear that any way had been found of making the crinoline more comfortable. It would have been better that it should have been left in all its pristine awkwardness.

The skirts being made very full at the sides and rather long in front, were, no doubt, difficult to walk in, unless propped out by a crinoline. Flounces were enormous, from fifteen to seventeen inches deep. The skirts were flounced up to the bottom of the short-pointed bodice, and the sleeves had not only frills at the wrist, but frills on the upper part. The basque-shaped bodice was worn a good deal, and if the steels of the crinoline were large at the top the effect was extremely ugly. The quantity of material used by these flounces induced economical ladies to adopt the plan of having stuff skirts to silk dresses, the beginning of the foundation skirts of later days.

In 1860 there seems to have been a great deal of controversy over the crinoline, and one writer suggested that rich women, who could afford to have freshly starched petticoats every day, should discard hoops, while women who could not pay a heavy washing-bill might still keep to their steels and whalebones. However, rich and poor alike continued to wear the crinoline up to the end of the sixties, in spite of intimations that it was going out.

Among the out-door garments which held an honoured place in the affections of this period was the black silk jacket. Everybody was wearing it, from little girls of ten to matrons of sixty. It began in 1855 as the casaque. This was a jacket-bodice for in-door wear. Then the casaque worn for a promenade costume was called a mantille. It was of *glacé* silk, tightly fitting, with a deep basque, and wide sleeves put in very low on the shoulder, as all sleeves were then. Afterwards, when the casaque came to be called merely a jacket, it was made both tightly fitting and loose, but always wide-sleeved and trimmed with frills, lace, or fringe. It was not so much the fashion then to walk out, even in summer, without some addition to the in-door costume besides the bonnet. But it was not at all necessary to have everything to match. Costumes *en suite* were not invented then. What is given in one of the fashion-journals as a "very handsome toilet" for

September, 1860, will be remembered by many as a typical costume of that time: "A green and white striped silk, flounced, wide sleeves, muslin under-sleeves and collar, black silk jacket flounced, and wide sleeves; grey straw hat with maroon velvet, cocks' feathers and Swedish gloves." It was in this year that the Empress Eugénie popularized clear white muslin, which had been rather superseded by other materials; and immensely wide *bouffant* muslin dresses were a good deal worn.

Plaids were in favour for a number of years. They were made in large and small checks, in woollen cloth, in Irish poplin, and in silk, and there were a good many cross-bar materials in light summer goods. But one of the most favourite stuffs for warm weather was alpaca. It exactly suited the style of dress and the taste of the time. Goods with a dull surface were not popular, and the bright, dressy-looking alpaca commanded universal approval. Women whose purses were not very long hailed it with delight. In winter French merinos were much used, bright blue and violet being great favourites. The partiality for striking colours was due to the fact that the neutral and indeterminate hues were then so wanting in tone and richness. They were dull without being soft. Think of the dispiriting shades of chocolate red, of the muddy unwholesome browns, and the indescribable greens, which were neither myrtle nor olive, and who can wonder that people preferred crude scarlet, violet, and grass green?

There was a keen taste for jewellery. People liked plenty of everything in those days, and when they had ornaments wore them all at once. Long gold ear-rings, set with coloured stones, each ear-ring as large as a good-sized shawl brooch, were thought the perfection of elegance. The elder women, who did not wear necklaces, consoled themselves by putting on two brooches, one at the throat and one at the bottom of their large lace collars. As wide sleeves were worn, bracelets followed naturally; and the bands of black velvet round the wrist were introduced as economical make-shifts for bracelets. They lasted a long time in fashion, for the black velvet made the hands look white. Coral ornaments, which are seldom seen now, were much in vogue.

About 1863, when "of trimmings it may be said that they are more desperate than ever," dress was at its meridian of ugliness. The skirts were wider, the mantles more overladen with gimp and fringe, the bonnets more pompous and aggressive looking. Morning gowns were made with loose, shapeless coat sleeves. The next year came the scarlet "Garibaldis," which were always "riding up," and required an agonizingly tight waistband to keep them in their place. Children had their frocks stuck out like little balloons, showing the frightful trousers; and they wore ugly buttoned boots, which tried the tempers of the nurses. Out-of-doors they were arrayed in long paletots, in which they looked prematurely old. Boys were ridiculous imitations of grown men.

The perennial question of tight-lacing was much discussed in 1863, when small waists threatened to become fashionable. Waists have always been held to be malleable and movable by the arbiters of fashion. Letters appeared in the ladies' newspapers strongly advocating the wearing of stiff, tight corsets at an early age, and praising the practice said to be in vogue at stylish schools of forcing girls to compress their figures according to a given standard. Even the sterner sex joined in defending tight corsets, if the letters were genuine. The model held up to admiration was the Empress of Austria, whose portrait appeared in the Exhibition of 1862, and who was the happy possessor of an exceedingly slender waist and graceful figure.

It does not seem, however, that, after all, there was much more tight-lacing at that period than before or after, the tendency being repressed by the waists becoming shorter, especially for full dress. Skirts continued enormously wide and fan-shaped. The crinoline was slow to disappear. If it went out of favour slightly in the winter, the flimsy muslins, which seemed to want something to keep them in condition, restored it in the summer. No one would have thought of wearing a muslin which hung softly round the figure. In 1866 a new kind of crinoline was introduced which could be easily folded. Stiff crinolines had long given place to stiff petticoats for evening wear, and as some objection was felt to wearing a great many petticoats, the ball dresses were made with several skirts that they might attain the proper proportions. The first skirt would be white satin, the next net, the third tarlatan—all plain—and lastly came the dress skirt itself, ruched and frilled. A tulle ball dress often had six skirts of tulle over a foundation of satin. Most of the evening dresses had small trains.

The next fashion was to gore the skirts in every width. It was an economical change, as a silk dress, instead of taking sixteen or seventeen yards, only took eleven or twelve. No steel crinolines were worn; they were all made of horsehair. Trains were very moderate, and were worn for smart promenades as well as evening dresses. Plain morning dresses were all short. It is impossible to chronicle all the minute changes which occurred up to the fall of the Empire and the crinoline together, to enumerate multifarious fashions which were only variations of one theme. By 1868, or thereabouts, the crinoline was practically gone. A council was held in Paris by the leaders of fashion anent the crinoline, and there was a good deal said in its favour. One of the arguments put forward for its retention was that the high heels of the shoes made women walk so badly they could not support the weight of their gowns without the crinoline. The conference ended in a compromise. The crinoline was modified into a petticoat, with some stiff bands round the bottom and up the back.

According to M. Challamel, the successive shocks which the crinoline had received were too much for its constitution, and it could not bear up against any fresh onslaught. A fashion which had lasted so long must inevitably have died out. "It disappeared; shall we say for ever? Do not some women regret the crinoline which gave them a certain presence?" M. Challamel's doubts have been too well justified. There are women who, if they are not old enough to regret the crinoline, would like to see it restored; and we can never be sure from season to season that some turn in the wheel of fashion will not bring it back. A mode so pronounced, if once set going, becomes very tyrannical. Every one who does not conform feels herself peculiar, and the number of non-adherents diminishes daily. Between the people who are really unable to judge for themselves, and the people who will wear anything rather than not be in the forefront of fashion, any absurdity is sure to win over a large number of followers. Fortunately, every year women are acquiring more liberty of action with regard to dress, and are realizing that, after all, disobedience to the mandates of fashion does not involve such terrible consequences.

CHAPTER IV.

1870–1893.

Style of dress after the fall of the crinoline—Narrow skirts—The Princesse robe—The Æsthetic Movement—The Woollen Movement—Rational dress—Changes in underclothing—Influence of modern customs on costume.

"Une mode a à peine détruit une autre mode qu'elle est abolie par une plus nouvelle, qui cède elle-même à celle qui la suit, et qui ne sera pas la dernière."—LA BRUYÈRE.

AFTER the fall of the Second Empire dress assumed a new form. There was a reaction from the balloon style of costume; but there was no return to the antique. It was not a revival of the classic modes which had prevailed at the beginning of the century, but an entirely new departure.

The change was not strongly marked until about the middle of the seventies. From 1870–1872, being a time of general mourning in France, there were no new modes invented. For a short time Paris ceased to be the arbiter of fashion, and Parisian modistes cast their eyes to London for fresh ideas.

In the pride of conquest, Germany made an attempt to assume the leadership, and, through the medium of the principal fashion-journal in Dresden, claimed the right to be the dictator in matters of dress as in politics. The Government are said to have distinctly favoured the idea, which was by no means beneath their notice. Paris, however, soon recovered herself, and before the year 1872 was out had regained her place.

After we had practically got rid of the crinoline, the modes which had been begotten and had flourished during its reign were still with us. Many people wore small crinolines in the early seventies, and in 1872 the newspapers were advertising a new kind of crinoline called the "Pagoda," presumably made like the pagoda sleeves, quite close at the top and wide just at the bottom. The majority who had given up crinolines wore their skirts very wide and bunchy, and made up for the loss of steel and whalebone by putting as much material as possible into their gowns. Wide, scantily gathered flounces gave place to closely kilted frills liberally disposed all over the dress—on the skirt, on the double skirt, on the sleeves, and on the bodice. Short waists were worn, and very unbecoming they were with those befrilled gowns. Out-door jackets were made with very short backs and very long fronts. Hats, which were more popular than bonnets, were heavily trimmed, and the hair was coiled and plaited over pads in a large chignon worn high. Ball dresses were elaborately decorated with flowers, and had long trains. Morning gowns were made long, and in the summer dresses cut a little open at the neck were worn out-of-doors. The pagoda sleeve was still fashionable; there were no really tight sleeves worn, but very simple morning dresses had the sleeves made a little closer at the wrist.

It was a great time for wearing dresses in two colours, an underskirt of one colour and a polonaise of another—an economical and convenient fashion which most people were sorry to see disappear. So much variety could be introduced at small expense, and old dresses and remnants used up to advantage. Indeed, the merit of this period was, that to be fashionable it was not necessary to be extravagant. There was plenty of variety in the form of dress, and plenty of licence as regards colour. Because your dress was in two shades of brown, nobody thought any worse of you for wearing a violet or a blue hat.

The Pompadour and its English equivalent, the Dolly Varden costume, came up in 1872, and were generally popular. However, these pretty, flowered gowns, being made in soft, thin materials, were only adapted for summer or evening dress. In 1873 a few bold spirits made an attempt to introduce long, plain skirts with no trimming whatever; but we were not to be emancipated from the burden of kilts and frills. Paris tried to induce us to part with the polonaise, but that attempt was likewise unsuccessful; and in 1874 we had the sleeveless polonaise as a new variety of that form of dress. It became more and more the fashion, especially for summer, to have costumes carried out in two colours. The mixtures were sometimes rather startling—or we should think so now—and there was an extraordinary liking for large bows and steel buckles, which were supposed to give a finish to the looping up of the polonaise.

It was about 1875 that dresses became narrower. The fulness was all gathered to the back; the front and sides of the skirt were drawn tightly over the knees, so tightly that walking was difficult. All dresses, except the plainest of morning gowns, had trains—some long and some short—which were trimmed with close kiltings. There was a good deal of drapery at the back. The form of dress was either a skirt and jacket bodice, a skirt and polonaise, or the Princesse robe made in one, but draped and kilted. The Princesse dress when not excessively narrow, was one of the mos becoming of all modern costumes, as it was one of the most original. It was not a revival of anything; it was not classic any more than it was mediæval: the Princesse robe was purely modern, the evolution of an age which was weary of crinolines and wide, flopping skirts. It was not perfect: to be effective it required to be made long, and was therefore unsuited for a walking-dress; the train was apt to be heavy, because so much trimmed, and the style was an extremely trying one to the stout and broad. But, in spite of these disadvantages, the Princesse robe remained in favour for a long period with women of all ages. In 1878 and 1879 it was the general form of dress, and every one who did not care to trust to the unreliable invention called the "dress suspender" walked about with the train in the left hand. It was not then considered admissible to let the dress sweep the pavement, as it has been since.

It was towards the end of the seventies that there arose in London two new movements in dress, both of which, although affecting at the time only certain sections of society, have had a distinct and lasting effect on costume. One was the Æsthetic Movement; the other the Dress Reform Movement. The Æsthetic Movement began with a coterie, who held heterodox views on art generally, and proceeded to carry those views into all matters of daily life. As far as they and their followers were concerned, they completely revolutionized the outer man. Dress, furniture, and surroundings underwent a total change. Houses were turned upside down by the votaries of the new movement. Carpets were taken up, and we had polished floors with matting and rugs. People who had long white lace curtains dyed them yellow, and sold their damask suites to make room for lounges and chairs of odd shapes and styles. Pier-glasses disappeared, and the mantel-pieces rose as if by magic. Blue china and pottery of all sorts were scattered about on shelves and brackets, and in every corner there was a vase with a sunflower or a lily. Peacocks' feathers played an important part in mural decoration. Colour began to have a new meaning. All sorts of previously unknown shades were introduced, and names had to be invented for these novel tints.

In dress the effect was startling. An æsthete was a being of a totally different order, whose costume was at complete variance with the conventional modes. It was loose and flowing in form, suggestive of ease, not to say indolence, and in colour it was subdued and indeterminate. A distinct preference was shown for what was irreverently called "greenery-yallery;" but dull blues, faded pinks, and coppery reds were also seen. Men did the best they could with unromantic coats and trousers, let their hair grow long, and wore limp collars and soft silk handkerchiefs for cravats. The women swept about in trailing gowns of the approved shades, made in the softest cashmere or Indian silk. The gowns were plain and narrow, very wide in the sleeves and low in the collar, over which fell a broad lace of creamy hue, while the throat was encircled with several rows of amber or Venetian beads. The hair was either in a loose knot at the nape of the neck or cut short and curled, and a heavy mass of curly, wavy hair hung over the forehead down to the eyebrows.

The æsthetes afforded abundant food to clever limners and versifiers, and numerous were the satires—good-humoured for the most part—of their ways and habits. At Oxford, where there was a knot of æsthetic undergraduates, ridicule took a more active form. Raids were made upon the rooms of the men who showed a harmless taste for art-serge hangings, blue china, and peacocks' feathers. These sanctums of æstheticism were sacked, and their owners were very roughly handled by the Philistines bent on giving a practical lesson to the lily worshippers. Some of those who affected æsthetic costume were assaulted, and had their long locks unceremoniously clipped. The æsthetes had their prototype in the eighteenth century, when there was a Florists' Club whose members worshipped the pink and the tulip instead of the lily and the sunflower, and would walk miles to see a new variety of their favourites and gaze abstractedly upon their perfections.

Although the Æsthetic Movement had its ridiculous side, though there was a great deal of unreal sentiment expressed, though people professed to be yearning and striving after the beautiful when they were only yearning and striving to make themselves peculiar and were craving for novelty, the effect has been good on the whole. The practical protest which it made against the use of crude colours resulted in a marked improvement in the hues of wearing apparel. The Movement gave rise to a general awakening of the colour sense. Some years previously there had been seen here and there artistic fabrics for furniture of quite a different order from those generally in use. Some came direct from the East, some were designed by clever colourists like the late Mr. Helbronner in this country. By degrees dress fabrics in these subdued tones followed. At first the result was not altogether pleasing. When the æsthetic craze was at its height all colour seemed to have faded out of costume, and people whose complexions needed a little warmth and richness clothed themselves in washy green and muddy orange. A good wholesome colour was voted barbarous. Gradually things righted themselves. The æsthetic public displayed more judgment, and as the demand for the new colours increased the hues were improved. Warm, soft-tinted cashmeres and silks began to be seen in shop-windows. Messrs. Liberty led the van in this particular, and helped materially to raise the standard of taste by the introduction of a new class of stuffs, softer and lighter in texture, and purer and richer in colour than those that had hitherto been worn. The beautiful camel's-hair cloth was imported from the East, and English dyers, resorting to the ancient mode of using vegetable dyes, produced a great variety of rich and delicate hues.

The Æsthetic Movement has influenced large classes of people who appeared to be outside its range. They modified their costume, insensibly, in accordance with the new ideas spread abroad. The æsthetic form of dress, although never a universal fashion, gave a strong impulse towards a simpler, more artistic style. Conventionality received a salutary shock. When some of the best-dressed women boldly disregarded the mandates of the modistes, and contrived to look well without the aid of tight corsets and heavily trimmed skirts, timid people who had been halting between two opinions ventured out of their rut. Fashion and æstheticism running side by side modified each other.

The Dress Reform Movement began about the same time as the Æsthetic Movement, viz. late in the seventies. It arose in Germany, and might more properly be called the Woollen Movement. An idea was started that wool was the only proper clothing for the human frame. Everything was to be of wool, even to the pocket-handkerchiefs; and all underclothing was to be of the natural, undyed wool. The Jaeger Company was started for the making of woollen garments, and soon there was quite a furore in Germany for woollen clothing. The Company had more orders than it could execute. Some of the articles found their way to England. At that time underclothing was in great need of reform. The usual wear was cotton, which was cold in winter and unhealthy in summer. Cotton garments when supplemented by flannel made underclothing bulky, and the style of the outer dress required that it should be close and compact. The soft, warm, natural wool was hailed with delight. It was just what people wanted. Every article that could be procured was sold directly. The goods could not be made fast enough to meet the demand. People went mad about wool. They slept in woollen sheets and clothed themselves from head to foot in wool. Regular "woolleners," who abjured silk, satin, muslin, and velvet gowns, had to renounce all festivities at which it was impossible for them to appear in woollen. No " woollener," for instance, could go to Court. But for ordinary occasions wool answered all purposes, as it was dyed in every shade and made in various qualities.

The majority of people were, however, content with woollen fabrics for underwear. There was such a rush for these garments that ladies would drive up in their carriages to the emporium in Mortimer Street, where the first agency was established under the management of Miss Franks, and carry off the precious bales without waiting for them to be wrapped up. Sick people fancied that woollen garments would restore them to health. One evening, during the height of the frenzy, two professional nurses drove up in a cab from Stoke Newington to procure night-dresses for an invalid. It was after business hours, and the shop was closed. Inquiring for the manager's private address, they tracked her to Haverstock Hill, and from Haverstock Hill to Camden Road, where they arrived about ten p.m., and, securing the coveted garments, drove joyfully back with their booty to their patient at Stoke Newington.

The subject of a new system of dress began to be much discussed. All the defects and vices of the existing form were commented upon minutely, and a fresh crusade was started—backed by doctors and sanitarians—against the old enemy, the corset. The advocates of the new system were radical in their reform. They insisted upon an entire change throughout. The leading feature, as every one knows, was the bifurcated garment. In 1881 an exhibition was held, and "divided skirts" were freely displayed on living models, who obligingly offered themselves for inspection. A few women contrived to wear the "rational dress," and to escape the lynx-like eyes of the street urchin. Others, not so fortunate, after a few trials, returned to their former modes.

On the whole, this attempted revival of Bloomerism, modified, had but a transient success. But the general movement in favour of lighter clothing, more equally distributed over the body, has been very serviceable. The barbarous condition of underclothing in the days of our grandmothers is marvellous to reflect upon, and one wonders that, in such a climate as ours, a more rational system was not invented before. Petticoats are not clothing—they are merely coverings; but to pile up petticoats, in varying numbers, according to the weather, was the approved method of underclothing up to very recent times. The maximum of weight with the minimum of warmth was the end achieved. At the present day nobody need be uncomfortable and over-burdened unless they choose. This is a great deal to have accomplished.

The Æsthetic Movement and the Dress Reform and Rational Dress Movements had much in common. They worked partly on the same lines. All three were opposed to the tyranny of fashion, were foes to corset and compression. All enjoyed a brief spell of popularity, and have since settled down to work on broader and less sensational lines.

The characteristic of modern fashion is a taste for extreme simplicity. No costume has been more popular than the tailor-made gown in which the limit of plainness has been reached. The tailor-made gown was begotten by the taste of the modern woman for sport. Adopted at first by a small circle, it was speedily taken up, and is now worn by all sorts of people who never saw a moor in their lives or walked on anything but a pavement. Imitations of the tailor-made gown are common, for the genuine article, simple as it looks, is an expensive luxury. The peculiarity of modern dress is that it becomes more costly as it grows plainer. There is nothing cheaper than smartness, but successful simplicity is only achieved at considerable cost, for every detail must be perfect. The example of the Princess of Wales has done much to foster the taste for simplicity. We are now less under the influence of Paris than formerly, owing to the new development English fashionable life has taken. Parisian ladies have been taking hints from us in this latter nineteenth century, and have learnt to rise early, to walk, ride, and hunt, and, accordingly, to dress *à l'Anglaise*, in short skirts and thick boots.

Side by side with this plainness there is a great deal of elaborate, gay dressing. The severe tweed morning gown is exchanged, in the evening, for the most gorgeous of ball and dinner costumes. "Young girls clothe themselves as their mothers did twenty years ago, in silks, satins, velvet, and brocade, while ordinary married women dress like princesses, and seek to outvie each other in the magnificence and variety of their costumes."

It is, perhaps, because morning dress has become so much plainer, because it is now chiefly confined to woollen and cotton fabrics, because it has been bereft of the adornment of jewellery, that evening dress has blossomed out into greater richness. People tire of being plainly dressed, and want some outlet for their fancy. The habits of the present day have contributed to a change in the style of dress among the middle classes. Those who would formerly have only dressed for the evening when they were going to receive or be entertained, now habitually change their attire for the family dinner, which is at seven instead of two. And they dress more elaborately. Full dress is considered necessary for small gatherings provided they take place after a certain hour. All entertainments are much later and more formal. Champagne and flowers appear constantly on dinner tables where years ago they were only rare visitors, reserved for birthdays and other special occasions.

Children's parties are no longer the informal romps they used to be, but carefully planned festivities with confectioners' suppers. Children's dress has certainly improved. Until recent times there were no special designs for children, or none of any merit. Little girls of eight or nine had their basqued bodices and pagoda sleeves, their polonaises and double skirts like their mothers. Now they have the daintiest and most comfortable of costumes, easy, shapely, and suited to their growing limbs. Juvenile costume has at last become both simple and pretty, and the choice is endless.

The great increase of luxury in the decoration

and furniture of houses has influenced costume. People must dress up to their surroundings. "Millionnaires spend fabulous sums on marble baths and painted ceilings, on parquet floors and carving and pictures, on Louis XV. furniture and copies of antique and expensive brocades." Smaller people follow suit as far as their means will allow. "The house beautiful has become the universal aspiration."* The whole standard of comfort has risen, and new wants have been created. The complexity of daily life is constantly increasing with fresh inventions and fresh temptations to ease and luxury. All the requirements of the toilet have multiplied in corresponding ratio. "Trousseaux are larger and more magnificent every year; people begin where their ancestors left off, and girls wear billowy lace petticoats and transparent under-linen heavily trimmed with Valenciennes lace, while their mothers are content with a frill or a tiny piece of lace, or even a few simple tucks."

Dress, while to outer seeming more simple, is really more elaborate. Prices are lower, but needs are more numerous and pressing because the changes of fashion are so rapid. A greater number of people now feel it incumbent upon them to keep up with the times. Formerly fashion was pretty

* Lady Violet Greville, *The Gentlewoman in Society.*

much confined to the minority who constitute what is called Society. The rest envied and admired at a distance, following only the general changes, but not concerning themselves about trifling details. Now, people who cannot afford to discard half-worn articles of attire because fashion has taken some new turn, have their gowns and bonnets unpicked and altered for every passing whim. To be fashionable is to be commonplace. The really distinguished thing is to be unfashionable.

CHAPTER V.

Court dress—Its contrast to fashionable dress generally—Festivities under the Regency—Abolition of hoops—Court dress in the Victorian era—Military dress.

> "Those that address kings must use silken words."
>
> "And why such daily cast of brazen cannon,
> And foreign mart for implements of war?"
> *Hamlet*, Act i. sc. 1.

THE closing year of the eighteenth century was very gay with balls and assemblies, and much more brilliance was observable in costume. Beau Nash describes the spring of 1799 as one of unusual splendour, and dress as flying from Greek simplicity to Eastern magnificence. In spite of the shadow caused by the King's malady, the fashionable world went on its way, and danced and gambled as usual. At Court the customary formalities were observed, and birthdays were celebrated with the same display of diamonds, lace, and embroidery.

It is curious to note the striking contrast which

Court dress presented to the dress of the fashionable world generally. Court costume had settled down into a stereotyped form. While narrow clinging draperies falling about the feet in loose folds were being worn everywhere else—in the Park, at assemblies, balls, routs, and dinners—ladies still went to Drawing-rooms in enormous hoop-petticoats. The rigidity of Court etiquette has always preserved decayed fashions.

In the first quarter of the century Court costume was very nearly approaching the grotesque. Conformably with the prevailing taste Court dresses were made with short waists, and short waists were not intended to be accompanied by hoop-petticoats. The effect of a hugely puffed-out skirt under a low and extremely short bodice was most disfiguring. If hoops were unsightly before, they became ten times more so then. In 1807 we find the bodice cut very low in front, with a ruff rising up at the back to a moderate height, the hoop very wide, and the train very narrow. The sleeves were composed of a single puff on the shoulder, gathered into a band with a frill of lace at the edge, and the long gloves left about two inches of the arm exposed. The materials for Court dresses that year were silk covered with Brussels lace, sarcenet draped with silver tissue, and embroidered crape.

The Princess of Wales had one robe made of silver tissue, embroidered with emeralds, topazes, and amethysts in the form of vine leaves and grapes.

At this period the ornamentation of the pocket-holes was a great feature in the costume, and on a Court petticoat there was quite a panel of embroidery on either side over the pocket-holes. Much ingenuity was displayed in embroidery, and the most elaborate patterns were devised and carried out with a great deal of taste. Queen Charlotte and the young princesses used frequently to embroider their own gowns, the Queen desiring to set an example of thrift to her ladies. Conventional designs were not so much seen as representations of natural objects, such as silver acorns, shells, roses, festoons of leaves in real silver, and peacocks' feathers with brilliants for the eyes. A birthday robe for one of the princesses was composed of silver tissue and Etruscan net, ornamented with laurel wreaths in silver foil, and "bouquets o chestnut blossoms with the kernel bursting from the shell."

Real pearl fringes were sometimes used. The Princess Amelia excited great admiration at one of the Drawing-rooms held in 1807, by appearing in a black net dress made over white satin and bordered with oak leaves and acorns in satin and chenille. The head-dresses were generally diamond bandeaux and ostrich feathers. But the most tasteful work could not atone for the unsightliness of the hoops, made the more prominent by the broad bands of richly coloured embroidery. The trains being so narrow, looked absurdly out of proportion to the rest of the dress, and did not relieve the width of the petticoat at all.

In 1808 the hoops were wider than ever, but the waist was longer, in fact almost in its natural place. No pointed waists were seen; they were all round, whether high or low. The contrast between a lady in Court dress and a lady arrayed for a fashionable party was so great that they seem to belong, not only to totally different periods, but to different nations. One of the fashion-magazines, in describing the birthday dresses of that year, prefaces its remarks by saying that the notice will be as brief as possible, as "this species of attire is of too high an order to be generally adopted,"—a fact for which the age should have been deeply thankful.

Feathers were worn very large and high in the earlier years of the century. There was little taste shown in the disposition of the plumes. The Princess of Wales, who, though she did not enjoy the reputation of her husband for perfect dressing, was, of course, regarded as a leader of fashion, wore large ostrich feathers rising straight up from the top of her head. The Queen, on one occasion, appeared in a head-dress composed of five hundred heron feathers, which had been presented to her by the Turkish ambassador. Ostrich feathers were generally used, but there were also worn the gorgeous plumes of the Bird of Paradise and feathers culled from the pheasant and the macaw. No ladies wore powder; but the hair was dressed high, in puffs and curls and loops.

Under the Regency, in spite of the personal unpopularity of the Regent, things went gaily in high places. There were very brilliant Drawing-rooms and receptions. In 1811, the first year of the Regency, there was a magnificent fête at Carlton House, the residence of the Regent, to which all the exiled French royal family were invited, together with the foreign ambassadors and the chief members of the nobility. The expense of this fête amounted to £15,000; and after it was over the public were admitted to view the scene of entertainment. The crush was terrific, and numerous accidents occurred. It was a money-making time for milliners, tailors, upholsterers, and purveyors of all sorts. As for the jewellers, their shops were literally ransacked, and diamonds were hired at ten per cent. Tunics and robes were laced with diamond chains, and fastened with diamond clasps and brooches. It was naturally the occasion for the display of the most splendid dresses; and as the edict had gone forth that the preference was to be given to British manufactures, all the ladies appeared in Spitalfields silks, Buckinghamshire lace, and Norwich crapes. Ireland was to the fore on this occasion, and supplied beautiful specimens of silver embroidery, the shamrock figuring prominently in the patterns. White satin, covered with shamrock embroidery in silver, made a very tasteful and splendid robe. Some of the dresses were embroidered in precious stones. The gentlemen were either in richly embroidered satin and velvet or in military or naval uniform.

When Princess Charlotte was married to Prince Leopold of Coburg, in 1816, there was another grand display, the Queen appearing in gold tissue and silver network, and the bride glittering in white llama and silver. The House of Commons voted ten thousand pounds for the Princess's wardrobe, and ten thousand for jewels, in addition to the grant of sixty thousand a year. Two years later there were the marriages of the Princess Elizabeth and the Dukes of Cambridge, Clarence, and Kent. The wedding-gown of the Duchess of Kent was of gold tissue, lined with white satin, and trimmed with llama and

Brussels lace; and that of the Duchess of Clarence was of silver tissue and lace. Pure white was not thought essential then for a bridal robe. In one respect bridal costume was more expensive, as bonnets were still much worn. A fashionable bride who was married in 1812 wore a bonnet that cost a hundred and fifty guineas, a veil worth two hundred, and a gown seven hundred guineas.

Pearls and diamonds were the regulation Court jewellery, and always used for necklaces and bandeaux, though all sorts of stones might be employed for garniture. At the coronation of George IV. the Duke of York wore a diamond cross which he hired of a jeweller, who sold it the next day to the famous Mr. Coutts for fifteen thousand pounds. Cornelian, especially white cornelian, was a favourite wear on ordinary occasions for a long period. A cross of white cornelian was considered to impart an air of becoming piety.

Hoops continued to be worn at Court up to the reign of George IV. It seems, however, that people were getting thoroughly tired of them, and that the milliners were less careful than when hoops were a universal fashion; for in 1818 there was a complaint in the *Lady's Magazine* of the "ill-contrived hoops" seen at the Drawing-rooms, and ladies were warned that a good effect could not be produced unless great attention were given to procuring a well-formed hoop. Certainly the strangely distorted petticoats of "ladies of quality" which are depicted in fashion-plates were much in need of better contriving.

When, at length, hoops were abolished by the good taste of George IV., the costumes worn at Drawing-rooms took the form of the fashions of the day. The clinging gowns were never seen at Court, for by the time the Court had left off wearing hoops the wider skirts were in fashion. In the reign of William IV. Court dress was pretty much the same as the full dress of the period, except for the trains and high feathers. The same may be said of Court dress during the Victorian era. From time to time modifications have been made in the cut and disposition of the train, in the size and shape of the sleeves, in the decoration of the bodice and petticoat, to accord with the modes of the day. The main features of the costume have, however, remained practically the same. The style of a Court dress cannot vary greatly. There must always be the petticoat, the train, the veil, and the feathers.

The anomaly of low dresses for an afternoon function like a Drawing-room is a survival of the time when low dresses were universally worn for all ceremonials and festivities. A few years ago permission was accorded to ladies who were delicate, and to whom the low dress meant great risk of illness, to wear their gowns cut square or even high; but a special order has to be obtained, and few care to avail themselves of the privilege which marks them out as singular.

The head-dress has been much improved. There are no huge, waving plumes standing out at frightful angles, or towering straight up like a parrot's crest, but three modest white ostrich feathers twisted prettily into the hair. Deftly arranged, with the long veil falling behind, they can be made to suit every face, and there is nothing so generally becoming.

It is interesting to look back to some of the records of the costumes worn by the Queen during the first year of her reign, 1837. For one of the State balls she wore "a white satin petticoat, over which was a silver llama tunic, trimmed with silver and white blonde lace *agrafé* on either side, with maiden-blush roses, studded in the centre with brilliants. The head-dress was of roses, the centre formed of brilliants, and a small bandelette confined the whole." For the banquet at the Guildhall on November 9th of the same year, her Majesty wore a pink satin robe shot with silver, and a tiara of diamonds. The Lady Mayoress seems to have been in Elizabethan dress, for she wore a large ruff and a stomacher one mass of opals and diamonds. She had a green velvet robe, lined with white satin, and bordered with Brussels lace, over a petticoat of llama and gold. At the prorogation of Parliament in 1837 the Queen wore the royal crimson velvet and ermine State mantle or robe over a white satin petticoat worked in gold. Her stomacher, bracelets, and tiara were all glittering with diamonds.

Under no circumstances, it seems, shall we ever be rid of the costly and inconvenient train, for therein lies the chief glory of a Court costume. The regulation length is twelve yards, which is a good deal for a woman to carry in addition to the complete dress. Etiquette imposes heavy burdens. Some trains are made to start from the waist, others from the shoulders, to which they may be either hooked or sewn. Trains are always of some rich, substantial material, whatever the rest of the costume may be. We never see trains made of silver tissue, trimmed with point lace, which used to be worn; they are all velvet, lined with satin or brocade; satin, lined with poplin or a contrasting shade of itself. Some twelve years ago almost every Court dress was made with a tulle petticoat, over a satin foundation, festooned with flowers; the bodice was very simple — cut quite low on the shoulders, and finished with a bertha of tulle; while the sleeves were, like babies' sleeves, one small puff. Now, tulle petticoats have quite gone out; and bodices, following the fashion of the day, are made with capes and big puffed sleeves.

The plainness which was creeping into all male costume invaded gentlemen's Court dress in the first half of the century. There were no more delicately coloured silk coats, but only plain, dark cloth. Waistcoats were still made of embroidered satin, and were cut much lower than the usual waistcoats. A dark brown coat, a white satin waistcoat, white cashmere trousers, and boots formed a very usual Court costume in the forties. The colour of the coat varied from year to year. At the present day the white satin waistcoat has given place to one of white marcella; the coat is invariably chocolate, with trousers to match, if trousers are worn, but knee-breeches and white silk stockings are much more general. The chocolate cloth suits are trimmed with gold lace and have gilt buttons. The alternative costume, and the one more commonly worn, is the black velvet suit, coat, vest and knee-breeches, black silk stockings, and shoes with steel buckles corresponding to the steel buttons on the coat. Sometimes a frill is made to the shirt, and sometimes the ordinary white tie is used; plain linen collar and cuffs are always worn. The cocked hat—the *chapeau claque*, which is carried folded under the arm, has undergone no variation in shape since the beginning of the century.

Ministers, consuls, members of the Royal Household, all have their special dress. Ministers are divided into five classes, the first-class ministers being distinguished by the quantity of gold lace embroidered on the breast of the coat, which is of dark-blue superfine cloth, single-breasted, and buttoned closely like a military coat, not showing anything of the waistcoat, collar, or cuffs. White kerseymere knee-breeches and white silk stockings complete the costume. The cocked hat is decorated with plumes. White kid gloves are worn with every class of Court costume except for mourning.

Gentlemen's Court dress, showy as it is in comparison with ordinary full dress, would, at one time, have seemed plain to the verge of impropriety. What would men of the last century, who wore diamond shoe-buckles, have thought of appearing in their sovereign's presence in cut steel? How scandalized they would have been at the idea of substituting a narrow band of plain cambric muslin for their beautiful Mechlin lace cravats! How indecent they would have thought the closely cut, uncurled, unpowdered hair! There is a difference, too, in the ladies' costumes; for although the velvets, satins, and brocades worn at Court are as rich as formerly, the lace and embroideries as delicate, and the diamond necklaces as splendid, there is less profusion of jewels. We do not garnish robes with precious stones, make borderings of amethysts, and fringes of pearls. Our ornamentation is less ostentatious. Drawing-rooms are not the occasions for such barbaric displays of wealth.

Military dress, in the early part of the century, was almost as cumbersome and elaborate as it had been before. Officers and privates alike were still compelled to submit to a style of coiffure which was only fitted for dandies. The long pigtail was worn up to 1804, when its length was reduced by seven inches. In 1808 an order was issued abolishing it altogether. But this did not release the soldier from the irksomeness of a daily visit from the hairdresser. It was still obligatory that the men should have their hair thickly powdered. Captain Gronow relates that, when he was a Guardsman, in 1813, the Duke of Cambridge one day gave him a severe reprimand because he had not the proper quantity of powder on his head, and threatenened to put him under arrest if he appeared in such a state again. On field-days the hair-dresser had to begin his operations at dawn; and if there were any festivities going on in the evening, the tedious performance was gone through again. It was about this time that the celebrated hair-dresser Rowland flourished. His charge for cutting hair was five shillings.

George IV. was exceedingly particular about the neatness of the soldiers' appearance. He used to say that a wrinkle in a coat was unpardonable, and consequently the men were squeezed into coats in which they could hardly move their arms.* In 1823 the Infantry were for the first time clothed in trousers and boots instead of breeches, gaiters, and shoes. But the Artillery Company seem still to have worn the long black gaiters with numerous buttons, which must have been very troublesome. Their uniform was blue, with scarlet and gold facings, and pipe-clayed belts. The question of time never seemed to be considered in the soldier's equipment. His comfort and convenience were sacrificed to what the authorities considered a good appearance.

At the coronation of George IV. the Household Brigade, for the first time since 1794, were seen glittering in steel cuirasses. During this reign the jackets of the infantry were made longer. The

* Luard, *History of the British Soldier.*

Guards wore such enormously high bear-skins that the sentry-boxes had to be altered to enable them to enter. But these bear-skins, which, in 1834, were decorated with long feathers, were so heavy that they fell into disuse, and a steel helmet was substituted. William IV. had a fancy for clothing the Army in scarlet throughout, with the exception of the Artillerymen and the Rifles. He also had the uniform of the Navy changed to correspond, and the white facings were altered to scarlet. After the accession of the Queen, the Navy went back to their original blue-and-white, and the Light Dragoons to their blue uniform. The 16th Lancers were still kept in scarlet, as a mark of special favour.

CHAPTER VI.

Changes in the costume of the commonalty—Dress of servants—Cheapening of materials—Apparel of the working classes: its unsuitability—Shams.

"Most think more about the fineness of the fabric than its warmth, and more about the cut than the convenience."—HERBERT SPENCER, *Education*.

THE progress of time has had a curious effect on the dress of the bulk of the people. Fashion among the richer classes has been continually reproducing old forms, but there have been no revivals of costume among the masses. Any characteristic dress once lost has never returned. At one period apprentices always wore blue coats and flat caps. That fashion went out with the general change of attire, and has not been recalled. Red cloaks used to be worn by women of the farming class and in the country districts generally. Red cloaks now are only seen in Wales. Workmen once wore sensible smocks, but they have long since taken to dirty unwholesome corduroy suits;

and though the old-fashioned smock is still worn in some country places, it has never been revived as a class costume. The modern spirit revolts at the idea of wearing any dress which denotes occupation. We still put our men-servants into liveries, which are tolerated because they are expensive and handsome, and the cost comes out of the masters' pockets. As a rule, the great army of male domestics which we maintain at such huge expense in England, to the astonishment of foreigners, take a great pride in their appearance. Their situations being so often a sinecure, they not unnaturally regard themselves as intended for ornament rather than use. Many of them probably share the opinion of the Bath footman who confided to Sam Weller that a good uniform was the only thing that made the service worth entering.

The position of female servants and the conditions of their employment have so entirely altered during the last fifty years, that it is surprising they can be induced to retain the cap and apron. But when off duty, they dress as nearly as possible like their mistresses. It is not so in other countries, and it used not to be so here. Servants who wore muffs and veils and kid gloves would have been laughed at as too fine for their work, and called finicking misses by their own class.

There are still a few mistresses of the stricter sort who, when they advertise for a housemaid or parlour-maid, add the words, "no fringe." In future, when the character of the domestic service has undergone a further change, and our houses are in the charge of out-door brigades, supplemented by one or two resident "helps," any one who should presume to try and regulate the personal appearance of those in their employ will probably find themselves left without any assistance whatever.

Servants' dress has changed with the cheapening of material and the development of the trade in ready-made goods. And as the quality of the dress has changed, so has the style. Years ago, when gowns were generally made with gathered skirts sewn on to the bodice, a waistband was thought an unbecoming vanity in a servant. At the present day servants wear not only waistbands but watches, and are careful to have the newest cut in sleeves and bodices.

The unsuitability of the dress of servants, and women of that class, is partly due to the fact that useful, hygienic clothing is dearer than the flimsy, smart-looking goods. It is impossible to buy really strong boots and shoes, with low heels, at anything like the price for which the fashionable, high-heeled boots are to be procured. Unshrinkable woollen underclothing cannot be bought for the same money as the cotton, lace-trimmed garments which find such general favour. Many of the things that servants most require are practically beyond their reach.

Nearly all trade costume has disappeared. The butcher, certainly, still wears his blue jacket, but his neighbour, the poulterer, goes about his work in a cloth suit like a draper's. Carpenters, cobblers, and others of the artisan class work in cloth clothes that cannot be washed, and which always look dirty and slovenly in consequence.

The appearance of the commonalty in their holiday garb is apt to be frowsy and tawdry. There is nothing real about it, from the imitation fur on the women's jackets to the imitation gold pins in the men's ties. Sham seems to have entered into the very core of their costume. Strictly speaking a great part of our dress is sham, but sham ornaments are more offensive than the shams which constitute clothing, like waistcoats with lining backs and silk skirts with cotton foundations. The extraordinary rise of the trade in imitations is responsible for much of the incongruous costume of the commonalty. They are tempted with all sorts of cheap goods bearing a superficial likeness to the real things which are quite beyond their means

Luxuries that were formerly the monopoly of the wealthy are now within the reach of every one—in spurious forms. This has caused a complete revolution in costume. The commonalty have no longer a costume of their own. Wrote George Crabb: "*Apparel* is the dress of every one; *attire* is the dress of the great; *array* is the dress of particular persons on particular occasions. It is the first object of every man to provide himself with apparel suitable to his station." Not so, now. It is the object of most men and women to provide themselves with apparel that shall *not* denote their station, but the station of somebody richer and better placed.

CHAPTER VII.

Trade and commerce—The silk manufacture—Rise of alpaca—Cashmere and Paisley shawls—Lace-making—The woollen trade—Linen—Cotton—The glove trade—Pins—Jewellery—Patriotism in costume.

> "Euch, ihr Götter, gehört der Kaufmann. Güter zu suchen
> Geht er, doch an sein Schiff knüpfet das Gute sich an."
> SCHILLER, *Der Kaufmann*.

THE great development of trade and commerce which has marked the Victorian era was undreamt of at the beginning of the century. It was not foreseen that agriculture would sink into utter insignificance as compared with manufactures. While we were still using only hand-looms, while we were dependent on horse-power for communication by land, and on sailing vessels for crossing the seas, industry and commerce were in their infancy. Every attempt on the part of inventors to substitute machinery for hand-work in textile manufactures met with the strongest opposition from the operatives. The improvement made on the power-loom by Cartwright's successors, in 1813-14, caused riots in Lancashire and Yorkshire. During the same period there were risings in the midland counties among the lacemakers and the stocking and ribbon weavers, and a great many machines were destroyed by violence. When steam-power was introduced into machinery the working-classes declared that the bread was being taken out of their mouths.

A similar spirit was shown when it was proposed to remove or lower the duties on foreign goods, and yet the effect of removing restrictions has been to give a stimulus to the home manufacture. In 1820 Mr. Huskisson declared that it was owing to our prohibitive system that we were so far behind the French in the manufacture of silk. Events proved the truth of the assertion. In 1823, while the silk monopoly was in full force, the value of the export trade was only £351,409; in 1832, nearly thirty years after the monopoly had been done away with, exports had reached the annual value of £1,551,846.

The strongest protests were made against admitting foreign silk, even with a duty of thirty per cent. In 1835 the Spitalfields weavers clamoured for the restoration of the old law. Monopolists insisted that English trade was declining. It was the same thing with regard to wool and cotton. Merchants and operatives alike demanded protection, and manufacturers prophesied commercial ruin. They could not realize that the old days were past, that trade could no longer thrive in swaddling bands, that the paternal government of mediæval times was totally unsuited to a nation that was fast becoming the leading mercantile power in the world.

The silk manufacture, though it never attained anything like the dimensions of the wool and cotton industries, went on steadily increasing all through the first half of the century. The fear of competition sharpened the wits of the manufacturers and gave rise to improved methods of work. A great deal of smuggling went on in silk, and a regularly organized system of fraud was carried on between the large importers and the landing waiters, who between them contrived to cheat the revenue of considerable sums. Silks of all sorts were much in demand, both the thin washing silks and the more substantial kinds. People who were not at all extravagant in their habits wore silk when we should now wear wool. As light silks were largely used for summer wear, and were easily soiled, the dyers did a good trade. So common was it to wear dyed silks that they were even said to have been seen at one of the Drawing-rooms in 1824.

Since 1860 there has been a great falling off in

the silk trade, both home and foreign. The consumption of raw silk has fallen from six million to two million pounds' weight yearly. France has suffered terribly, for Lyons used to send us great quantities of silk. Between the years 1881 and 1887 the rate of consumption went down in England, France, and Italy, the difference in the United Kingdom amounting to about one million pounds' weight, as compared with the years 1861–1870. Germany, Austria, Spain and Switzerland have, on the contrary, shown an increase in their consumption. Quite recently, however, there has been a revival of the Spitalfields industry.

Fashion has had much to do with the ups and downs of the silk trade. While crinolines, wide skirts, and a *bouffant* style of dress were in vogue, silk held its ground. It was always much in request, and the stiffer the better. As long, too, as fashion remained in a comparatively quiescent state, silk was in favour with a larger class, for nothing stood so much wear and tear, and at the same time looked so well, as a good silk. All through the fifties the changes of fashion were unimportant. It was quite possible for quiet people to keep their dresses on from year to year without looking *outré*. But when styles vary from season to season with great distinctness the majority prefer cheap goods, frequently renewed, to more expensive and lasting ones. During the last thirty years changes have been much more rapid and pronounced.

The invention of new materials is another element which has contributed to the decline of the silk trade. A formidable rival to silk, as well as to other goods, was alpaca. In 1836 Titus Salt began to operate on the unpromising alpaca wool brought to Europe four years before from Buenos Ayres, and, after repeated attempts, succeeded in weaving it into a saleable cloth. It was the substitution of a cotton warp for a wool warp that was one of the most important steps in the new manufacture. Imperfect as were the early productions of the Bradford looms, they at once struck the popular fancy; and as the fabric was from year to year improved, the sale went up steadily. Alpaca was found an excellent substitute for the light summer silks. It was cheaper and more durable.

In 1844 the Queen ordered some of the new material. It was made from the fleeces of two alpaca sheep which had been imported to the home farm at Windsor. One of the articles manufactured was a piece of black-and-white plaid alpaca, which was so lustrous that it was difficult to distinguish it from silk. Another was a dress-piece in which the warp was rose-coloured silk and the weft white alpaca. By this time Salt had discovered how to combine alpaca with cotton, silk, and other wool in the most dexterous ways. Her Majesty highly approved of the articles submitted to her, and the inventor's fortune was made. The alpaca trade revolutionized the home markets; a new town sprang up as the seat of the manufacture, and hundreds of families grew prosperous on alpaca.

So things went on until about twenty years ago, when taste changed. Fashion decreed that gowns were to be close and clinging, to fall in easy folds. Soft woollen Cashmeres from the East were introduced, and all materials that were smooth and pliable came into favour. Alpaca began to lose ground. Nobody cared any more for lustrous, shining goods. For the last ten years there has been practically no demand for alpaca as a dress material, though for linings and other inferior purposes it is still used. A blight has fallen upon the once prosperous little town of Saltaire, and ruin has been brought to many homes. Considering the direction fashion is now taking, it seems possible that the alpaca trade might be to some extent revived. Soft materials will go out of favour, and there will be a demand for goods with plenty of "dress" in them, if skirts become any wider and stiffer.

Early in the present century muslin was still popular, as it had been in the last century. Nearly all the muslins worn by fashionable folk were Indian muslins. Sarcenet, chaly, crape, and other goods of light texture were in favour. We hear something, too, of Irish poplins, of Dalmatian cloth, and of rep. The home manufactures, though improving, were unable to compete with the more highly finished foreign goods, and France, Italy, and the East supplied the rich with most of their clothing materials.

It was about this time that the famous Indian shawls made in the Valley of Cashmere were imported. These shawls, which had also been brought to France, were so popular that the French manufacturers began to try and copy them. At first the experiment was tried of importing the Thibetan goat, but after the animal had been acclimatized with great difficulty, the wool was found to be so inferior to that of the goats dwelling in their native country that the attempt was given up, and the wool imported instead. The French workmen acquired great skill in this imitation manufacture, and before 1830 the sale of the shawls made in France was very large.

Our Norwich manufacturers, anxious not to be outdone by the French, proceeded in their turn to try and produce Cashmere shawls, but they were very inferior to those of our ingenious neighbours, and Norwich abandoned shawls and returned to more profitable occupations.

Then Paisley took up the idea, stimulated thereto by the desire to do something to atone for the decay of its muslin trade. Paisley was more noted than any town in Scotland for good spinning and weaving. The Cashmere yarn was imported from France at great cost, and some very successful copies of the Indian shawls were turned out. Yorkshire came to the aid of Scotland with a new Saxony yarn, which was called Thibet cloth; and Paisley and Bradford uniting their forces, Yorkshire making the centres and Paisley the borders, the imitation was perfected. The popularity of Paisley shawls was immense. In 1834, about four years after the invention of the Thibet cloth and the combination with Yorkshire, the value of these shawls amounted to a million sterling. Thirty years later shawls ceased to be fashionable walking-garments, their place being taken by mantles of silk, velvet, and cloth, and in 1874 the manufacture had fallen to a tenth of its former value.

The lace industry is one entirely dependent on fashion. In the seventeenth and eighteenth centuries an immense deal of lace was used by wealthy people, by men and women alike. Men have now discarded lace with other luxuries of dress; and tulle, net, and transparent materials generally, have largely supplanted lace in women's costume. The invention of machinery reduced lace-making from a species of art to a mere mechanical operation, and threatened to extinguish hand-work. At the time of the Queen's marriage there were so few skilled workers left in Devonshire that there was some difficulty about getting sufficient hands for the making of her Majesty's wedding-gown. It was composed of Honiton sprigs, and the pattern was immediately destroyed. The cost was £1000. The same piece of lace was used for the drapery of the the wedding-gown of Princess Beatrice in 1885. Honiton has always been the great lace centre of the west of England.

Early in the century a lace factory was set up at Tiverton by the lace-machine inventor, John Heathcoat, who had been driven from Loughborough, where his machines were destroyed by the Luddite rioters. Encouraged by the success of Heathcoat's invention, a Nottingham man, Levers, devised a new machine for making lace, and the Nottingham lace trade became very important. The older hand-made lace seems to have been thicker than the more modern lace. Miss Catherine Hutton, writing in 1818 about three generations of wedding-lace shown her by a friend, describes the newest as quite cobweb-like in appearance compared with the first. They were complete suits of lace, partly of point and partly of Brussels lace.

The quantity of cheap, machine-made lace now in use is enormous. But it is chiefly of the narrow kind, meant for trimming. Real lace is a costly luxury. The imitations, however, are so good, the patterns being so beautiful and the texture so fine, that it is sometimes difficult to distinguish machine from hand work. Still, this is not a lace period like the eighteenth century.

What were called caterpillar lace veils were made in the early part of this century. An ingenious officer of engineers, residing at Munich, devised a method of making caterpillars spin lace. "Having made a paste of the leaves of the plant on which the species of caterpillar he employs feeds, he spreads it thinly over a stone, or other flat substance of the required size. He then, with a camel-hair pencil dipped in olive oil, draws the pattern he wishes the insects to leave open. This stone is then placed in an inclined position, and a considerable number of the caterpillars are placed at the bottom. A peculiar species is chosen, which spins a strong web; and the animals commence at the bottom, eating and spinning their way up to the top, carefully avoiding every part touched by the oil, but devouring every other part of the paste. The extreme lightness of these veils combined with some strength is truly surprising. One of them, measuring twenty-six and a half inches by seventeen inches, weighed only 1·51 grains, a degree of lightness which will appear more strongly by contrast with other fabrics. One square yard of the substance of which these veils are made weighs four grains and one third, whilst one square yard of silk gauze weighs one hundred and thirty-seven grains, and one square yard of the finest patent net weighs two hundred and sixty-two grains and a half." *

The enormous addition to the population during the last fifty years, and the increase of wealth have, of course, brought about a correspondingly higher consumption of materials generally. All textile manufactures have trebled. Wool has branched out into many new directions. Invention has been busy with fresh patterns and fresh combinations of colour. There has been a remarkable increase of fine woollen cloths which have largely taken the place of cotton and linen goods for summer

* Charles Babbage, *On the Economy of Machinery and Manufactures.*

wear. Though fashion has caused fluctuations in the demand for particular classes of goods, the woollen trade as a whole, dealing with the necessaries of life, has steadily progressed. At one time reps, corded cloths, and other heavy materials with a harsh surface, were worn universally. Then came in a taste for smooth-surfaced Cashmeres. These were succeeded by soft, hairy materials, equally warm and of a much lighter make. English manufacturers have had to learn to compete with the Eastern weavers whose productions flooded the market. Rivalry and new machinery have brought about marvellous improvements.

One of the most popular clothing materials of modern times is the camel's-hair cloth, which is quite a unique cloth, not easily imitated by the use of Australian or South American sheep's wool, which makes such excellent woollen cloth. The camel's hair, which can hardly be called a wool, is now brought over undyed at a great saving of money.

Homespuns and tweeds have enjoyed a long run of popularity, and while formerly the thick, heavy tweeds were only used for men's apparel, the changes of fashion have brought them into requisition for women's costume. The travelling mania has considerably affected the clothing trade.

Every woman now has her tweed travelling costume, and for general wear tweed has, to a great extent, superseded other materials. The last few years have seen a change with regard to colour. Plain coloured cloths have been at a discount as compared with stripes and checks. Mixtures of indefinite patterns and indeterminate shades have been more used than anything else. Certain materials have completely gone out. Does any one now see a satin cloth or " Russell cord "—materials which were largely manufactured twenty years ago? Book muslin has disappeared in like manner, and so have *glacé* silks.

During the last half-century there has been a decline in the consumption of linen; and prices have fallen. In 1840 the amount used was nearly double what it is now. After the invention of the flax-spinning machine, at the end of the eighteenth century, the linen manufacture assumed a new phase. Spinning-mills were established in various northern towns, Lancashire and Yorkshire being the chief centres of the trade. It was at Barnsley that the white duck formerly used for smocks was made, and the Barnsley manufacturers early learned to rival the Scotch and Irish in the making of fine linen sheetings and damask. In Ireland the introduction of spinning by machinery gave a tremendous impetus to the linen manufacture. It was the foundation of the prosperity of Belfast. About 1828 Ulster was exporting yearly one million pounds' weight of yarn, and in 1832 Dundee exported more linen than all Ireland put together; but by 1865 the exports from Belfast alone had reached twenty-eight million pounds. At first only the coarser kinds of linen were produced by machinery; but as improvements grew up, finer yarns were made, and the cambric branch of the linen manufacture was developed. By 1854 Ulster had thirteen thousand looms for weaving cambric, about two-thirds of the material produced being for pocket-handkerchiefs. A great commotion arose in the first quarter of the century, through the fraudulent practices of certain manufacturers who substituted cotton for linen warp; and for many years goods which were half cotton were passed off as pure linen flax.

In Scotland the Act for the stamping of linen, passed in 1727, was repealed in 1823, after much agitation, both manufacturers and merchants finding the stamping very troublesome when trade grew to large dimensions. At that time the value of the linen manufacture was reckoned at one million. Thirty years later it was estimated at ten millions. The American War of 1861 gave an impetus to the trade of the three Kingdoms, as no linen could be imported from America; but the benefit was merely temporary.

For clothing purposes linen has been largely superseded by cotton. Formerly, linen was universally used for underwear; but cotton, being cheaper and warmer, took its place. More recently cotton has been overthrown in favour of wool and silk. The hygienic clothing movement has diminished the consumption of white goods, to the great improvement and simplification of dress. The present generation clothes itself in flannel, natural wool, or silk, according to taste and means. At the same time there is a great deal of fine *lingerie* in use, and among the poorer classes coarse cotton underclothing is worn because it is cheaper and stronger than anything else.

Cotton, unlike linen, has gone up in the last fifty years. The cotton manufactures of Great Britain are said to be equal to the aggregate cotton manufactures of all other European nations,* though we have lost the overwhelming supremacy we once enjoyed.† Up to the time of the cotton famine in 1860, which caused such a terrible loss to English manufacturers, the cotton trade had been going up by leaps and bounds. The American War, which

* Mulhall.   † Fox-Bourne.

brought prosperity to the linen trade, had the reverse effect upon the cotton trade. However, in spite of that check and of subsequent trade depressions, the quantity of cotton produced has increased, on an average, at the rate of one hundred million yards a year.* Our cotton is exported to all parts of the world. It takes the first place among our textile manufactures.

Cotton enters very largely into clothing materials where we do not expect to find it, being mixed with wool and silk in all sorts of cheap goods. It is the foundation of velveteen. Cotton is a necessary part of so many fabrics, that the variations of fashion cannot affect its consumption as they affect the consumption of silk, for instance. There has been a greater demand lately for pure woollen goods; but for the cotton mixtures, which are cheaper, there is always a large market. Some of the daintiest materials, such as worked muslins, are made of cotton; and in excellent coloured cotton goods there are now such endless varieties that these fancy stuffs have taken the place of silks. Every year sees a larger development of this branch of the cotton industry.

The smaller clothing trades, like the larger, have been revolutionized during the present century.

* Fox-Bourne.

For some time after the introduction of cutting and sewing machines the glove industry resisted the new movement, which substituted machine for hand work; but invention triumphed eventually, and the manufacture of gloves became an automatic process. But what affected the glove trade above all was the removal of the heavy restrictions on imported gloves, which took place in 1826. The first result was a large increase in the number of operatives, as the master glovers made great efforts to develop their manufacture in view of the foreign competition. The import duty on skins having been reduced, they were able to buy larger quantities of the raw material. Over-production followed, with the discharge of many workers, and much consequent discontent with existing legislation. There were loud complaints against the facilities afforded to the ingress of foreign goods. But when, in 1835, an inquiry was instituted into the glove trade, it was found that, in spite of the outcry against French gloves, fifteen times as many gloves were made in England as were imported.

After a period of depression things began to mend, through the energy of the glovers in extending their manufacture in those directions where they had least to fear from competition, viz. in the making of strong, stout gloves, especially leather gloves. The immense demand in modern times for kid gloves, which are now worn by all classes, has caused quantities of gloves to be sold as kid which are really made of other skins. The superiority of French gloves is due to the sedulous care with which the kids are reared, so that their skins may be soft and delicate.*

Recently fashion has turned from thin, fine kid gloves to those of a thicker and more durable kind. The dull Swedish kid gloves for a time commanded the market; and silk, lined and unlined, has been a formidable competitor to *glacé* kid.

The glove trade is very dependent on fashion. If sleeves are long, gloves are short, and *vice versâ*. Light-coloured kid gloves for day wear have very much gone out of use. At one time gentlemen were all wearing lemon-coloured kid for morning dress, and ladies wore light gloves with dark costumes. Now, gentlemen seldom wear light gloves, except for evening dress; the tan-coloured gloves are more worn than any other sort; and, as for the old-fashioned plain black kid, they are kept entirely for mourning. Ladies, on the contrary, wear black kid a great deal; and all dark shades are preferred for morning dress, except with very light costumes. The best gloves still command good prices; but

* Beck, *History of Gloves.*

the trade in cheap gloves has developed greatly. Gloves can be had at almost any price, and the custom of wearing gloves has extended to classes who formerly dispensed with those additions to costume.

The pin trade has likewise undergone a complete change. In 1812 there was an unsuccessful attempt to produce pins by machinery. At the present time there are machines which turn out two hundred pins a minute, and the manufacture of pins goes on at the rate of fifty millions a day, three-quarters of which are made in Birmingham. The term "pin-money," dating from a period when pins were of sufficient value to be ranked as separate items, seems to have puzzled foreigners a good deal. They thought we were inordinate consumers of pins when they heard that a lady of fashion was allowed one thousand pounds a year by her husband for "pin-money."

Gold and silver wire-drawing is not a new industry. It dates back some four hundred years. Here, again, machinery has taken the place of hand-labour in the working up of wire into braid for military embroideries and epaulettes. Fashion has had a good deal to say in the matter of jewellery, though the art of the goldsmith and jeweller has not been subjected to any violent changes during the last hundred years. New forms of setting precious stones have been introduced, and every now and then certain classes of ornaments become fashionable and disappear again. Coral and silver have ceased to be generally worn, at least in the forms in which they were used years ago. The application of enamel to jewellery, which was practised in the Middle Ages, was revived in this century, and had a run of popularity. The value of precious stones varies from time to time. During the last forty years there has been a great rise in the price of rubies, as much as eight hundred pounds being now given for a single ruby that would, formerly, not have fetched more than two hundred pounds. Fewer ornaments are now worn by the middle classes. Ear-rings have gone out of use everywhere, and there is hardly any jewellery seen with morning dress. Cheap jewellery has multiplied exceedingly, but in that the fashions are very evanescent.

One of the most recent attempts at reviving British trade by what may be called "forced means" was made in 1881–82, when there was a depression in the woollen industry. It will be remembered how the Marquis of Salisbury, at a meeting held in the Mansion House, entreated the public to patronize goods of British manufacture;

how the Countess of Bective set the fashion for wearing home-made fabrics, and for a time the shop windows were full of materials labelled " British ;" how merry the Press were over the new craze and the patriotism that would voluntarily make use of articles which were " British, inferior, and obsolete." From time to time similar efforts have been made on behalf of certain Irish industries, and a good deal is being done by the energy of private individuals to develop the domestic manufactures of Ireland.

Trade is now worked on totally different lines from those which served at the beginning of the century. The old methods are worn out. The fierceness of competition has developed an elaborate and expensive system of advertising, on which manufacturers and merchants are, practically, dependent for success. Consequently, few can stand alone. A business, as soon as it becomes large, passes from the hands of the individual to those of a syndicate or company. It is an age of big combinations, and those who either cannot or will not fall in with the new order of things are frequently left behind and crushed.

CHAPTER VIII.

CONCLUSION.

"Life for delays and doubts no time does give,
None ever yet made haste enough to live."
COWLEY.

It is natural to deem our own century more important, more full of interest than any other; to look upon our discoveries, inventions, improvements, as greater than those of our forefathers; to regard our attainments in science, literature, and art as far surpassing theirs; to consider our education and culture as the best that England has ever seen. Every age, enriched with the experience of the one before, has been justly proud of its superior advantages and its consequent advance. Every age has thought it was living at a prodigious rate compared with its predecessor. Every age, too, while on the one hand vaunting its pre-eminence, has, with cynical self-depreciation, lamented the benefits enjoyed in the past.

The nineteenth century, as Mr. Besant truly

says, actually began with steam and railways, the electric telegraph, and the development of the Colonies. Until we had these and many other things, we were still part of the eighteenth century. The old ways, customs, social habits of the first forty years of the nineteenth century were those which it had inherited. It did not acquire any individuality until a third of its term was gone. But all that time it was growing and ripening, preparing to burst forth into that vigour, fulness, and multiform development which it has shown since. So rapid and so many have been the changes in every department of life, so complete has been the transformation of our mental attitude as well as our outer seeming, that to go back a hundred years seems like taking a leap into some half-forgotten mediæval period, when there was time for everything and room for everybody, and men were not deafened by their own noises and dazed by their own activities.

We of the second half of the nineteenth century are children of another age, and have little in common with the men of the first half of the century. We neither eat nor drink, do our business, take our pleasure, fight our enemies, nor make love, as did our grandfathers. And neither do we appear as they did. Our costume betokens our changed habits and occupations. Cut-away coats, dinner jackets, tailor-made tweed gowns and Ulsters signify a period of rapid movement, haste, and high-pressure. It is only a section of society that has time to dress. The rest are merely clothed. Especially does this apply to men, whose costume has been reduced to something like a uniform. With her usual vehemence, Ouida recently remarked of male attire that it was "the most frightful, grotesque, and disgraceful male costume which the world has ever seen. When the archæologists of the future dig up one of our bronze statues in trousers they will have no need to go further for evidence of the ineptitude of the age."

The whole conception of what is fitting with regard to male dress has changed. To excite attention by any remarkable richness of apparel is considered vulgar and ridiculous. Sumptuous attire is now only thought fit for barbarians. It has become impossible for a gentleman to wear very costly clothes. He cannot carry more than a moderate sum on his back and maintain his position and dignity. At one time he could wear a fortune on his coat, and be all the more honoured and respected. But the luxuries that a gentleman could once indulge in are now denied him. The laws which bind him to keep to a certain style of costume are inexorable, though unwritten. Lace, for instance, which once formed such an essential aad expensive feature in the wardrobe of a man of fashion, is absolutely tabooed. In velvet—except for Court costume—the utmost that he is allowed is a modest collar. Silk and satin he can have nothing to do with except as linings and facings. In jewellery he is limited to watch-guards, studs, scarf-pins, and rings, the latter worn very sparingly. The ideal which a gentleman sets before himself is not elegance, but strict conformity with the recognized mode. To be as like his fellows as possible, so that no one should be able to discover any individuality in his costume, seems to be the aim which he sets before himself, and, in most cases, successfully achieves. The man of business and the man of pleasure are at one in this.

The keynote of modern costume is adaptation. We have attire for every function and amusement. The etiquette of male costume is rigorous. A man would as soon think of appearing on the Stock Exchange in "tweeds" as of attending a garden-party in a dress coat. Members of Parliament observe or used to observe certain rules with regard to dress, which have, however, lately been broken in upon by the new men. The morning lounger in the Park, the afternoon promenader, have each their special toilette, slight as the difference may appear to the uninitiated.

The simplicity which has taken possession of men's costume has also invaded women's dress, in a lesser degree. Cheap travelling, the opening up of new employments for women, the changed ideas with regard to the physical education of girls, the modern out-door recreations and games, the rush of the leisured classes into all kinds of social and philanthropic work, have all contributed to revolutionize costume. Women have fashioned their dress to their occupations and amusements, or rather are trying to do so, for we are yet a long way from success. In the last century no fashionable lady possessed a pair of thick, double-soled, leather boots. She never walked out in wet weather, and would have fainted at the idea of climbing a mountain. Now she walks about in all weathers, tramps over the moors, and scales the Alps. In the early Victorian period the only kind of physical drill was the back-board; there was no tennis, even the mild diversion of croquet had not been invented then, rowing was thought unladylike, and the mere mention of cricket or golf would have scattered all the proprieties to the four winds. Now girls have their gymnastic costumes, their tennis frocks, and their boating flannels like men.

At the beginning of the century there were no women engaged in the higher departments of commercial life; a needy gentlewoman, if she were not qualified to become a governess, earned a bitter livelihood as companion, or starved on fine needlework and water-colour sketches. There were no trains to catch, there was no rushing to and fro every day between city and suburb; women were compelled to find their occupations at home. They took little or no part in public work: their philanthropy was confined to visiting the poor in their own neighbourhoods; there were no women's "movements," no clubs, and very few of those active organizations for ameliorating life in which women are now the chief workers.

It is true there were complaints of women seeking and obtaining fame in the walks of literature. A clamour was raised against them for invading the rights of man. History, philosophy, politics, poetry, and the drama were menaced by authors in straw bonnets and muslin gowns, grumbled the critics of that period. Lawyers and bishops trembled lest their provinces should also be invaded. What would they think now, those worthies of 1800, if they could see how society has changed? At the present day women are as much abroad as men; they are in the professions, in all kinds of business, in the midst of the great current of social activities, which sweeps along at a constantly increasing speed. Their life has entirely changed. And this applies to women of all classes, from the artisan's daughter to women with landed estates and old titles. Ladies of rank have become shopkeepers; girls whose mothers were domestic servants are clerks and book-keepers; women who pride themselves on belonging to the "people" sit on committees with countesses.

All this has brought a rigorous plainness into costume. Muslin frocks are only seen at garden parties, except in the country; silk has given place to the more serviceable woollen materials; and light colours are eschewed for obvious reasons of fitness and economy. Everything for daily use must be quiet and unnoticeable, able to stand wear and tear, rain and dust, tumbling and creasing. The omnibus and tram-car have much to answer for in the toning down of our costume from gay to grave. In these democratic days everybody rides in public vehicles, and this custom not only tends to produce a sober uniformity in dress, but is a great bulwark against any huge extravagance of fashion. "Constructed to hold twelve inside" would be a meaningless mockery if six out of the twelve wore large crinolines.

The facilities for locomotion create a sameness

in costume. The railways carry to remote parts of the United Kingdom all the modes of the Metropolis. Our country cousins, when they come to London, are unnoticeable except by their better complexions; they are as well posted up in the fashions as the residents of Mayfair. Provincialism in dress has been swept away. One county is as like another as two pins. We have, consequently, lost a good deal in variety.

Women, like men, in their anxiety to avoid being thought peculiar, are parting with individuality. There is a conventional contour about the women of to-day which any striking fashion makes more decided. When the round-faced and long-faced, the rosy and the pale, the fair and the dark, the tall and the short, the stout and the slender, all adopt the same style of coiffure, the same cut of gown, the same colours when particular shades are put upon the market, they are forced into bearing a delusive likeness to one another. This kind of resemblance, noted by Viollet-le-Duc among women in the fifteenth century,* being purely artificial, becomes tiresome and monotonous. It takes away the impress of personality from costume. There is no occasion to reduce ourselves to a dead level of uniformity. "Il y a autant de foiblesse à fuir la

---

* Cf. *Reign of the Roses*, vol. i. chap. iii.

mode qu'à l'affecter," but it is quite possible to put some character into costume and yet escape eccentricity, to conform to fashion without becoming mere puppets.

A plea was recently put forth in a periodical publication for more colour in our streets. Men contribute nothing by their costume; and on wet days, when the richer tones of women's dress are all hidden under dull-hued cloaks, the effect is very lugubrious. The writer humorously suggested that emerald green, scarlet, and orange should be used for mackintoshes and umbrellas. It is not impossible that this should come to pass; colour is entirely a matter of fashion. Shades are adopted, not because they are really preferred, but because some unknown arbiter decrees that such and such colours shall be worn. Many people learn to like a colour they once thought hideous, if it becomes the mode. But we do not, as a nation, habitually use bright, glowing colours; they look harsh in our hazy atmosphere, and do not accord so well as neutral tints with the English type of face and complexion. Colour, too, needs very careful disposition and combination, and we are not strong in the æsthetic sense. We are safer, therefore, in keeping to indeterminate shades.

Neutrality is coming more and more to be the

basis of costume. Both class dress and provincial dress have been practically abolished. "Mere insistence on costume for purposes of discrimination must go on disappearing; the more marked a fashion, the more promptly is it imitated and subsides. When it is the test of a lady or gentleman to avoid extremes, extremes must diminish. Increase of education or improvement in ordinary comforts diminishes the taste for extremes."

It is a taste that belongs essentially to a barbaric age. Men begin as savages with bright paint and grotesque ornaments. While yet untutored they prefer the costume which is most striking, most extreme, and measure a man's dignity and importance by the pronounced character of his dress, by its brilliance and elaboration. Little by little the conception changes, and appropriateness is more esteemed than display. When a higher stage of culture is reached, costume is regarded as a setting, a frame for the picture, and whatever would be likely to attract undue attention is suppressed. We cease to desire to be distinguished by our clothes; we study to make them harmonious, part of ourselves,—to so arrange the details of form and colour that a perfect proportion is produced, and no one part dominates over the rest. Because we often fail in doing this we follow Fashion wherever she leads, hoping that we may some day stumble into the right path. Too much is trusted to apparel; it is placed on too high a pedestal. The body is made subservient to the clothes, forced into some sort of conformity with arbitrary designs founded on misguided fancy. We have believed—we still believe—that costume can do the impossible, can reverse the decrees of Nature. We forget that costume is Nature's adjunct; that it can only be successful when it follows on her lines. Men and women are born each with a different form and colouring, it may be very imperfect; but it is better to bow to the inevitable, to adapt the attire to that shape and those tones of colour, than to resist, and vainly strive by adventitious aids to obliterate the characteristics of the physique. A plain face is made all the plainer by very rich apparel. Sumptuousness is the handmaid of beauty.

There are some people whose instinct always guides them to the right choice, who are never at fault, whatever the vagaries of fashion. It is because they have learnt the secret of leaving off at the exact point where appropriateness ends and exaggeration begins. Those people never follow fashion slavishly. Fashion deludes the judgment and causes the imagination to run wild. It is, as Mr. Gladstone said, a wheel "going round and round, always puzzling you, like a fireworks wheel, but always landing in a total negation of progress, and with a strong tendency to the substitution of mere caprice for the real pursuit of beauty."

THE END.

www.ingramcontent.com/pod-product-compliance
Lightning Source LLC
Chambersburg PA
CBHW020230240426
43672CB00006B/474